# SRI

*Translation by*

**SWAMI NARAYANANANDA**

Published by

**THE DIVINE LIFE SOCIETY**

P.O. SHIVANANDANAGAR—249 192
Distt. Tehri-Garhwal, Uttarakhand, Himalayas, India
www.sivanandaonline.org, www.dlshq.org

First Edition: 1972
**Seventh Edition:** **2019**
[ 1,000 Copies ]

©The Divine Life Trust Society

ISBN 81-7052-092-4
EO 4

PRICE: ₹ 95/-

Published by Swami Padmanabhananda for
The Divine Life Society, Shivanandanagar, and printed
by him at the Yoga-Vedanta Forest Academy Press,
P.O. Shivanandanagar, Distt. Tehri-Garhwal,
Uttarakhand, Himalayas, India
For online orders and Catalogue visit : dlsbook.org

# SRI GURU GITA

DEDICATED TO
**SRI GURUDEV
SWAMI SIVANANDAJI MAHARAJ**

# FOREWORD

Homage unto the Almighty Lord. Worshipful adorations and prostrations at the Holy Lotus Feet of Beloved Gurudev Sri Swami Sivanandaji Maharaj and all the Brahma Vidya Gurus. May the Grace of the Lord, who is the Guru of Gurus, Jagadguru, the choicest blessings of worshipful Guru Maharaj and all the Brahma Vidya Gurus be upon all the devotees.

In spite of much that has been told and written on the concept of the Spiritual Guru, still there exists a great deal of confusion and misunderstanding in the minds of many seeking souls.

This book "GURU GITA" with original verses and lucid commentary in English undoubtedly serves not only as a great boon to dispel at once the confusion and misunderstanding of all such sincere aspiring souls but also infuses in them unflinching faith and devotion towards their Guru which is the fundamental prerequisite for attaining the Supreme Bliss. Above all, the Real Nature of Sadguru, which is akin to the nature of the Supreme Being, is very beautifully depicted in this great book "Guru Gita" which unfailingly serves as a beacon light to all those sincere seekers who are already treading the spiritual path.

May this valuable book have widest possible circulation and benefit all the spiritual aspirants and devotees.

O beloved seeker! I sincerely urge you to make a little daily reading of this "GURU GITA" an unfailing part of your spiritual Sadhana and daily Svadhyaya programme. And, once a week, upon every Thursday, please make a complete reading of the whole of "GURU GITA" as your special Sadhana for that day of your Guru. Reflect deeply, meditate seriously with one-pointed mind and realise that Great Guru who is eternally shining in the inmost recess of your heart.

May your daily devout reading of a portion of this scripture serve to purify your heart, illumine your life and make you shine with spiritual radiance.

Gurudev Sri Swami Sivanandaji's blessings accompany this book.

Jai Sri Sadgurudev!

Om Namo Bhagavate Sivanandaya.

—Swami Chidananda

# THE SUPREME IDEAL

(By Brahmanishtha SRIGURU Swamigal,
from one of his inspired talks)

A thinking person in the course of his life experiences a mental crisis, when the world and worldly life fails to satisfy him and he begins to think that there must be a higher purpose than mere vital and mental existence and that there must be something positively True and Good behind all this. He therefore naturally uses his intellect and turns to philosophy for help and guidance.

Philosophy is ultimate by its very nature, a search for the Absolute, first for the Absolute Truth as distinct from mere appearance, and afterwards for the Absolute Being, the source and explanation of all dependent existence. Philosophy gives the rational explanation of things and explains why they exist. It uses reason as its means. It proceeds as far as reason can go and has to stop short; and it posits three objects: God, Nature and Man, as the explanation of the Universe and as constituting it. There it halts, as it cannot solve or explain the relation between these three.

Now, here steps in Religion and gives solution of the relation between God and Man. This solution is both subjective and objective. On the objective of ethical side, Reason and Philosophy help man to formulate his right conduct. But on the subjective side, they fail and cannot solve the problem. This gap is filled by Religion which starts with the two distinct principles of Faith and Revelation.

Faith in God is the first postulate, and acceptance of Revelation the second postulate, and when we admit these two principles, we feel a strength and confidence in our quest of God.

By faith is meant the recognition of an object which is neither present in consciousness nor discovered by the senses. As God cannot be an object of the mind or senses, it is only by faith that man can link himself to him. When man tries to know God, he feels the need for the scriptures, which are the revealed authority, as coming from God and having the power to show the path to know him.

Now, the thinking person comes to the stage of realising the necessity of studying the Scriptures and understanding their meaning with a view to know God.

To understand what the scriptures teach, we require the instrumentality of reason and ratiocination.

This reason is the God-given power of understanding, and it has its own limitations; it has to be used therefore within the limits of authority and accepting only such data as are furnished by the Scriptures. These data are based on Revelation and are beyond Reason and have to be admitted on faith, as authority.

Using our reason in this manner, we acquire knowledge of what the scriptures teach. Knowledge is the product of our intellectual activity, whether it be perception, comparison or reasoning. It supposes a being who knows, an object known and a relation between the knowing being and the known object.

This relation occasioned by the mind's activity is knowledge. The ultimate principles upon which knowledge rests are incomprehensible and inexplicable: they cannot be known, they have to be believed.

Proper understanding of the scriptures gives us a knowledge of God and the relation of man to God, both of which are derived from Revelation. This is Theology as distinct from Philosophy which is pure reason.

Regarding the knowledge of God, there is the Mystic school, which believes that God may be known face to face, without any intermediate factor, by intuition or inspiration. There are cases of people in all religions, who have been such mystics and have vouched for experiencing God and known Him or seen Him face to face. This process is a yielding to the sentiment awakened by the idea of the infinite and a running up of all knowledge and all duty to the contemplation and love of Him. This mysticism despairs of the regular process of science and believes that it may attain directly, without the aid of the senses or reason and by immediate intuition, the real and absolute principle of all truth—God.

But such people are rare and exceptional. They form the extraordinary few, the geniuses in the field of religion, and they can be no example for the ordinary seeker after God with his normal faculties or power.

Thus, the thinking person starting with philosophy which posits the absolute and points to God, comes to religion which shows him the relation of his commands, and he links himself to God. Then, by the use of his reason, he acquires that right knowledge, which will lead him to the direct realisation or the experience of the immanence of God in him.

Applying these general principles which are common to all religions, we have the following guiding principles as our "Ideal".

The Ideal of man's life is to attain MOKSHA or freedom of the spirit. By Moksha is meant liberation from the cycle of births and deaths. And this liberation comes only when man or the Jiva gets ATMA-JNANA or self-knowledge. Until then, he is subject to births and deaths.

The JIVA has 3 faculties: The Indriyas (senses), the Manas (mind) and the Buddhi (intellect).

When the JIVA uses any of these three with reference to God,

(1) Whatever is done by the Indriyas is Karma;

(2) Whatever is thought by the Manas or contemplated is Upasana; and

(3) Whatever is known or understood by the Buddhi is Jnana.

The former two will not directly give Atma-Jnana but only the third, and it is therefore rightly held that salvation is gained only by knowledge.

This knowledge can be acquired only by the study of the Shastras (scriptures), which describe Brahman and the way to know it.

The Shastras say that the fittest person to acquire Brahman-knowledge is the Sannyasin who has transcended Karma and Upasana and is concentrating all the powers of his intellect in understanding what the Shastras say. There will thus be no diversion of energy or attention and his higher mind will move in one direction only.

But in the case of other persons who cannot give up fully mental or sensory activity and who yet are interested in the objects of the outer world, Shastras must also be studied, by means of which, in course of time, the knowledge side may become more and more strong and wean him away from his mental and sensory activities, so that he may become fit for entire practice of higher knowledge.

Hence (1) Faith, the God-given gift to man, in the revealed Scriptures, (2) Right knowledge as taught by the Guru and, (3) Service of the Guru are the only three means for the direct experience of delight in the Bliss of the Supreme Being, or what is termed "Brahman", in the Upanishads.

This is the path to Self-revelation. That is to say, experience is just the process of knowledge realising itself or becoming the essence of the ultimate reality.

In other words, to "Know Thyself" is to "Become Thyself" and "Be Thyself".

# SRI GURU GITA

# SRI GURU GITA

## CHAPTER I

अचिन्त्याव्यक्तरूपाय निर्गुणाय गुणात्मने ।
समस्तजगदाधारमूर्तये ब्रह्मणे नमः ॥१॥

1. Prostrations to Brahman, the Unthinkable, the Unmanifest, beyond or above the Gunas, (Sattva, Rajas and Tamas), the Self of the Gunas, the supporting Substance or Substratum behind the manifested universe.

|| ऋषय ऊचुः ||

सूत सूत महाप्राज्ञ निगमागमपारग ।
गुरुस्वरूपमस्माकं ब्रूहि सर्वमलापहम् ॥२॥

2. The Sages said: O Suta, the wise one, who has acquired thorough mastery over the Nigamas and

Agamas! Please narrate to us the real or true nature of the Guru, which has the power to remove all impurities.

*Notes:* Agamas are the Vedas and the Nigamas are texts dealing with rituals and injunctions contained in the Hindu Sastras. In the word 'Guru', the syllable 'Gu' stands for darkness and 'Ru' for the removal of darkness.

यस्य श्रवणमात्रेण देही दुःखाद्विमुच्यते ।
येन मार्गेण मुनयः सर्वज्ञत्वं प्रपेदिरे ॥३॥

3. By hearing which, man becomes free from all pains and by treading which path the sages have attained the state of Omniscience.

*Notes:* The query continues and goes upto the sixth verse.

यत्प्राप्य न पुनर्याति नरः संसारबन्धनम् ।
तथाविधं परं तत्त्वं वक्तव्यमधुना त्वया ॥४॥

4. By attaining which, man comes never again to the round of birth and death; please narrate that to us now, which is the Supreme Truth.

गुह्याद्गुह्यतमं सारं गुरुगीता विशेषतः ।
त्वत्प्रसादाच्च श्रोतव्या तत्सर्वं ब्रूहि सूत नः ॥५॥

5. O Suta, we are desirous of hearing all that and we are eager to hear them from you and particularly the Guru Gita which is the essence and secret of all secrets.

इति संप्रार्थितः सूतो मुनिसंघैर्मुहुर्मुहुः ।
कुतूहलेन महता प्रोवाच मधुरं वचः ॥६॥

6. Thus repeatedly prayed by the sages, Suta spoke these sweet words with great enthusiasm.

## SRI GURU GITA

*|| सूत उवाच ||*

शृणुध्वं मुनय: सर्वे श्रद्धया परयामुदा ।
वदामि भवरोगघ्नीं गीतां मातृस्वरूपिणीम् ॥७॥

7. Suta said: O Sages, hear with rapt attention. I shall now narrate to you the song (Gita) which is capable of destroying all the ills of the Samsara (the cycle of transmigratory existence) and which is like the mother unto you all.

*Notes:* The conversation between Lord Siva and Parvati is introduced by a question by the sages to Suta at the sacred spot Naimisaranya where the 18 Puranas were recited in days of yore.

पुरा कैलासशिखरे सिद्धगन्धर्वसेविते ।
तत्र कल्पलतापुष्पमन्दिरेऽत्यन्तसुन्दरे ॥८॥

8. Once upon a time, on the mountain peak of Kailasa (the abode of Lord Siva) frequented by the Siddhas and Gandharvas, and in the most beautiful place adorned by nature with shrubs, flowers, fruits, etc.

*Notes:* Siddhas are perfected beings. Gandharvas are experts in music in the heaven world.

व्याघ्राजिने समासीनं शुकादिमुनिवन्दितम् ।
बोधयन्तं परं तत्त्वं मध्ये मुनिगणे क्वचित् ॥९॥

प्रणम्रवदना शश्वन्नमस्कुर्वन्तमादरात् ।
दृष्ट्वा विस्मयमापन्ना पार्वती परिपृच्छति ॥१०॥

9 & 10. Seated on a tiger-skin, and surrounded by Suka and other saints, on one occasion, while Lord Siva was expounding to the Rishis the Supreme Truth, Parvati

(the consort of Siva) with Her face full of devotion, seeing the Lord bowing to some one with great fervent reverence and being very much surprised at this, asked the Lord thus.

*Notes:* Kailasa, the seat of Lord Siva, is the venue of Satsanga for the Rishis and saints as they often visit the abode of the Lord to pay their respects and be benefited by his instructive talks of advice.

।। पार्वत्युवाच ।।

ॐ नमो देव देवेश परात्पर जगद्गुरो ।
त्वां नमस्कुर्वते भक्त्या सुरासुरनरा: सदा ।।११।।

11. Parvati said: Prostrations unto Thee, O Lord of lords, Thou art the teacher of the whole world. Thou art Supreme. Thou teachest the knowledge of the Supreme. Gods, demons and men always worship Thee with devotion.

विधिविष्णुमहेन्द्राद्यैर्वन्द्य: खलु सदा भवान् ।
नमस्करोषि कस्मै त्वं नमस्काराश्रय: किल ।।१२।।

12. Lord Brahma, Lord Vishnu, Indra and others prostrate to Thee always, I wish to know who will be the recipient of Your prostrations.

Is there any one superior to You to whom You have to prostrate? Are You not the one Supreme Being, the sole abode or refuge of all prostrations?

*Notes:* This indicates that Goddess Parvati had noticed the Lord prostrating to someone during His prayers or at other times. In the celebrated Sri Ramcharitamanas, Saint Tulasidasji also brings in a similar instance and a doubt is raised by Sri Parvati.

Parvati was confirmed in the view that Lord Siva was the Highest and the Supreme Lord of all lords. This act of the Lord was a surprise to Her.

दृष्ट्वैतत्कर्म विपुलमाश्चर्यं प्रतिभाति मे ।
किमेतन्न विजानेऽहं कृपया वद मे प्रभो ॥१३॥

13. Noticing this act of Yours I am struck with great wonder. I am unable to understand this. O Lord, please enlighten me.

*Notes: Vipulam* means abundance or frequently done.

भगवन् सर्वधर्मज्ञ व्रतानां व्रतनायकम् ।
ब्रूहि मे कृपया शम्भो गुरुमाहात्म्यमुत्तमम् ॥१४॥

14. O Lord, O knower of all Dharmas, O Sambhu, please narrate to me the glory of Guru (preceptor) which is the best of all Vratas.

*Notes:* By using the plural it is indicated that Lord Siva is the knower and the authority for all Dharmas (duties) e.g., duties of students, householders, forest-dwellers, anchorites, ladies, the different orders—Brahmins, Kshatriyas, Vaishyas, Sudras, etc., etc. As such He must know the importance of the preceptor also. *Uttama* indicates that it is the best.

केन मार्गेण भो स्वामिन् देही ब्रह्ममयो भवेत् ।
तत्कृपां कुरु मे स्वामिन्नमामि चरणौ तव ॥१५॥

15. By adopting which particular method can an individual soul attain the supreme state of Brahmanhood? I prostrate to Thee. I worship Thy feet. Kindly explain this to me.

*Notes:* Worship of the feet of the Lord is Padapuja. Worshipping the feet indicates humility and receptivity on the part of the student. The Purusha Sukta says, *"Padosya Visva Bhutani*—the entire universe is but one foot of the Lord." So, if you worship the feet of the Lord, you worship the entire humanity and the world, the same effect is there by the worship of the Preceptor also. The importance of this will be revealed in various verses of this book.

इति संप्रार्थित: शश्वन्महादेवो महेश्वर: ।
आनन्दभरित: स्वान्ते पार्वतीमिदमब्रवीत् ॥१६॥

16. Thus repeatedly prayed for by Parvati, the great Lord Mahesvara (Siva—the Lord of lords) spoke the following words, His heart overflowing with abundant joy.

*Notes:* Teachers derive the maximum joy and happiness when eager seekers put pertinent questions. The heart of the teacher always seeks for sincere students. That is the reason for their joy. It is but natural that one gets joy when he gets what he wants. A thirsty man is satisfied with water, the hungry man with food. But teachers are satisfied when they get suitable and deserving students to whom they can unburden their knowledge. Without a deserving student the teacher feels the burden of his knowledge and considers his efforts fruitful when the students eagerly question and practise the precepts.

॥ श्री महादेव उवाच ॥

न वक्तव्यमिदं देवि रहस्यातिरहस्यकम् ।
न कस्यापि पुरा प्रोक्तं त्वद्भक्त्यर्थं वदामि तत् ॥१७॥

17. Lord Mahadeva said: O Devi, this is the Secret of all secrets. This is not to be revealed to any one. I have never divulged this to any one so far. But I shall tell you because of your great devotion to me.

*Notes:* Great truths are not divulged to all and sundry. But to the qualified disciples the teacher in his overflowing love and kindness reveals such secrets. The disciples serve the Masters and they in turn reveal these secrets. But never to one who is not a Bhakta such secrets are revealed.

*Tvadbhaktyartham:* This may be interpreted in two ways. To create devotion in you I reveal this, and also, because you are highly devoted I reveal this to you.

*Rahasyatirahasyakam:* There are some secrets which may be ordinarily revealed to select persons but there are certain secrets which can be revealed only to the dearest person. One such secret is this, that the Lord is going to reveal to Parvati. As long as teachers do not get such exceptionally qualified aspirants they do not divulge these secrets. They remain always as secrets only.

मम रूपासि देवि त्वमतस्तत्कथयामि ते ।
लोकोपकारक: प्रश्नो न केनापि कृत: पुरा ॥१८॥

18. O Devi! You are my own Self in another form. No one else has put me this question. This question of yours will benefit the whole world. Therefore, I shall narrate this to you.

*Notes:* The World-Mother, interested as She is in the welfare of humanity, has put this question. The entire humanity is dear to Her. Who else can be the well-wisher of a child if not the mother? There is no equal to the love of the mother in this world. Everything else comes next to this.

यस्य देवे परा भक्तिर्यथा देवे तथा गुरौ ।
तस्यैते कथिता ह्यर्थाः प्रकाशन्ते महात्मनः ॥१९॥

19. He who is supremely devoted to the Lord and has the same equal devotion to his Guru, to him alone will the truths explained herein clearly reveal themselves.

*Notes:* This verse appears in the end of the Svetasvatara Upanishad and hence is quoted by the Lord as Pramana.

This verse tells us the extent of devotion we should have towards the Guru. There is no difference between the Guru and God. Only when this Bhava becomes fully ingrained in the mind of the disciple, his spiritual progress becomes easy and sure.

यो गुरुः स शिवः प्रोक्तो यः शिवः स गुरुः स्मृतः ।
विकल्पं यस्तु कुर्वीत स नरो गुरुतल्पगः ॥२०॥

20. He who is the Guru is Siva Himself, so declare the scriptures, and the fact that Siva is the Guru, is reminded to us in all the Smritis. He who makes any distinction between the two, is guilty of the crime of uniting with his own preceptor's wife.

*Notes:* This verse gives the importance of the Guru and his identity with Siva, and tells us that it is an unpardonable crime to find difference between the two as in the illustration given above in the second half of the verse.

दुर्लभं त्रिषु लोकेषु तच्छृणुष्व वदाम्यहम्
गुरुब्रह्म विना नान्यः सत्यं सत्यं वरानने ॥२१॥

21. The Guru is Brahman and no other than Brahman Itself, O Parvati. I declare this Truth to you. Listen to my

words and believe, for this Truth is unknown to any one else in all the three worlds.

*Notes:* Durlabham means "Rare". It refers to the declaration "Guru is Brahman". The Guru who is really qualified and who is capable of imparting the knowledge of Brahman is rare. He is attainable with difficulty and by the Grace of God particularly.

वेदशास्त्रपुराणानि चेतिहासादिकानि च ।
मन्त्रयन्त्रादिविद्यानां मोहनोच्चाटनादिकम् ॥२२॥

शैवशाक्तागमादीनि ह्यन्ये च बहवो मताः ।
अपभ्रंशाः समस्तानां जीवानां भ्रान्तचेतसाम् ॥२३॥

22 & 23. The Vedas, the Sastras, Puranas, the Itihasas etc., the science of Mantras, Yantras, Mohana, Ucchatana, etc., cults like the Saiva, Agama, Sakta, etc., and other cults existing in the world today are merely false theories expressed in corrupted words which confuse the ignorant and deluded Jivas.

*Notes:* The concluding part of this verse appears in the succeeding verse. As it is, it looks like a condemnation of the different Sastras which is not the purpose of these verses.

The scriptures quoted here, are the different authoritative books of the Hindus on which Hinduism takes its origin, and the different cults they have given rise to.

जपस्तपो व्रतं तीर्थं यज्ञो दानं तथैव च ।
गुरुतत्त्वमविज्ञाय सर्वं व्यर्थं भवेत्प्रिये ॥२४॥

24. Japa, austerities, observances, pilgrimage,

sacrifice, charity—all these become a mere waste without understanding the Guru Tattva.

गुरुबुद्ध्यात्मनो नान्यत् सत्यं सत्यं वरानने ।
तल्लाभार्थं प्रयत्नस्तु कर्तव्यश्च मनीषिभिः ॥२५॥

25. O Parvati, I declare unto Thee, with all the emphasis at my command, that there is no difference between the Guru and the Atman (Self). Therefore, efforts should be made by seekers, men learned in the scriptures, men of wisdom, for its attainment.

*Notes:* The attainment of a qualified Guru is the only means to the attainment of Jnana. Therefore there is no difference between the Guru and Atma Jnana.

गूढाविद्या जगन्माया देहश्चाज्ञानसम्भवः ।
विज्ञानं यत्प्रसादेन गुरुशब्देन कथ्यते ॥२६॥

26. The hidden ignorance, absence of the knowledge of Self, the world, Maya, the body—are all caused by ignorance (Ajnana). By whose grace one attains direct knowledge of the Self—he is known by the name 'Guru.'

यदंघ्रिकमलद्वन्द्वं द्वन्द्वतापनिवारकम् ।
तारकं भवसिन्धोश्च तं गुरुं प्रणमाम्यहम् ॥२७॥

27. I prostrate to that Guru, whose two lotus-like feet help the removal of all miseries arising out of the pairs of opposites and who saves one from the round of births and deaths.

देही ब्रह्म भवेद्यस्मात् त्वत्कृपार्थं वदामि तत् ।
सर्वपापविशुद्धात्मा श्रीगुरोः पादसेवनात् ॥२८॥

28. I shall tell you that, by which the embodied soul,

purified from all sins, becomes Brahman. It is by the service of the Guru's Feet. I say this because of my special interest in you.

*Notes:* Service of the Guru includes physical service, learning and teaching of the Sastras and all acts which please him and particularly by spreading the teachings of the Guru among the eager and qualified aspirants.

An ideal disciple finds no difference between the Lord and his Guru. Worship of Guru is worship of God. Worship of God is worship of Guru. Those who find any difference cannot have real devotion to God and Guru.

सर्वतीर्थावगाहस्य संप्राप्नोति फलं नर: ।
गुरो: पादोदकं पीत्वा शेषं शिरषि धारयन् ।।२९।।

29. By drinking the water after washing the holy feet of the Guru and sprinkling the remains on the head, man attains the fruit of taking bath in all the sacred waters of all sacred rivers and of all pilgrimages.

*Notes:* Faithfully following the spirit of the teachings contained here, one attains the fruits mentioned. It is not exaggeration or praise. What has the Lord to gain from the ignorant Jivas of the world by misleading them?

शोषणं पापपंकस्य दीपनं ज्ञानतेजस: ।
गुरो: पादोदकं सम्यक् संसारार्णवतारकम् ।।३०।।

30. The Padodaka (water collected after washing the Guru's Feet) of the Guru has the power of completely burning up the filth of the disciple's sins, brightening the lamp of wisdom and taking him across the ocean of Samsara.

अज्ञानमूलहरणं जन्मकर्मनिवारकम् ।
ज्ञानवैराग्यसिद्ध्यर्थं गुरुपादोदकं पिबेत् ॥३१॥

31. One should drink the feet-washed-water of the Guru for the uprooting of ignorance, to end the cycle of Karma, birth, death, etc., and for the attainment of dispassion and knowledge of the Self.

गुरुपादोदकं पानं गुरोरुच्छिष्टभोजनम् ।
गुरुमूर्ते: सदा ध्यानं गुरोर्नाम्न: सदा जप: ॥३२॥

32. One should always repeat the name of the Guru, meditate on his form, drink the feet-washed-water and eat remnants of the Guru's food-plate.

*Notes:* All these practices constitute one-pointed devotion and his Ananya Chintana. It is complete dedication of one's life to his service only.

स्वदेशिकस्यैव च नामकीर्तनं
    भवेदनन्तस्य शिवस्य कीर्तनम् ॥
स्वदेशिकस्यैव च नामचिन्तनं
    भवेदनन्तस्य शिवस्य चिन्तनम् ॥३३॥

33. The repetition of one's Guru's name becomes the repetition of the names of Lord Siva, who is Ananta (the Infinite), and the meditation on the name of one's Guru becomes the, meditation on Siva.

यत्पादरेणुर्वै नित्यं कोऽपि संसारवारिधौ ।
सेतुबन्धायते नाथं देशिकं तमुपास्महे ॥३४॥

34. The dust of whose Feet helps to definitely bridge up the ocean of Samsara, such a saviour, Satguru, I daily worship.

*Notes:* Desika means the Demonstrator or Teacher who explains and points out the Truth to our intellect, so that we may properly and precisely understand the fact in our experience.

यदनुग्रहमात्रेण शोकमोहौ विनश्यत: ।
तस्मै श्रीदेशिकेन्द्राय नमोऽस्तु परमात्मने ॥३५॥

35. By whose blessings alone two evils of sorrow and delusion are destroyed, to that Supreme Lord Saviour Guru I prostrate.

यस्मादनुग्रहं लब्ध्वा महदज्ञानमुत्सृजेत् ।
तस्मै श्रीदेशिकेन्द्राय नमश्चाभीष्टसिद्धये ॥३६॥

36. With whose blessings man sheds off the great shackles of ignorance, my prostrations to that Supreme Teacher (Lord Saviour), who bestows all the desired objects including the four Purusharthas (Dharma, Artha, Kama and Moksha).

काशीक्षेत्रं निवासश्च जाह्नवी चरणोदकम् ।
गुरुर्विश्वेश्वर: साक्षात् तारकं ब्रह्मनिश्चय: ॥३७॥

37. The place where the Guru lives is Kashi Kshetra and his feet-washed-water is Ganga. The Guru is Lord Viswanatha personified and his words indicate the Taraka Brahma.

गुरुसेवा गया प्रोक्ता देह: स्यादक्षयो वट: ।
तत्पादं विष्णुपादं स्यात् तत्र दत्तमनन्तकम् ॥३८॥

38. The service of the Guru is Gaya-Kshetra, his body is the imperishable banyan tree (Akshaya Vata), his

feet, the feet of Lord Vishnu and anything offered at his feet bestows infinite merit.

*Notes:* To the ideal Guru-Bhakta, who has one-pointedness in devotion and who is established in the faith, Guru is Brahma, Guru is Vishnu and Guru is Siva, and the different places of pilgrimage like Kashi, Gaya, etc. There is no Tirtha or Punyakshetra other than his Guru. He sees Kashi, Gaya, Mathura, Vrindavan, Vaikuntha, Moksha, everything, in his own Guru. This sort of Guru-Bhakti is very rare and cannot be obtained without His Grace.

गुरुमूर्तिं स्मरेन्नित्यं गुरोर्नाम सदा जपेत् ।
गुरोराज्ञां प्रकुर्वीत गुरोरन्यं न भावयेत् ।।३९।।

39. The disciple should always meditate on his Guru, he should ever repeat the Guru's name, he should always carry out the behests of the Guru. He should be devoted to his Guru only and think of none else.

*Notes:* What is meant here is that for purpose of spiritual guidance and Sadhana the Sadhaks should have devotion to one Guru only. Satsanga and the gaining of knowledge of the Sastras and such other acts are not ruled out. When the truth is grasped nicely, the necessity for indefinite search for other Gurus ceases.

गुरुवक्त्रे स्थितं ब्रह्म प्राप्यते तत्प्रसादत: ।
गुरोर्ध्यानं सदा कुर्यात् कुलस्त्री स्वपतिं यथा ।।४०।।

40. Brahman resides in the mouth, i.e., tongue or Saraswati Nadi of the Guru, and the disciples attain Brahman by the Grace of the Guru. One should meditate on his Guru at all times, just as a devoted wife would think of her husband only.

*Notes:* Refer to Sloka 43 below. Brahma resides on the tip of the tongue of the Guru and his speech therefore contains Brahma or Chit-Ananda Nectar. *"Brahmananda-Rasa-Anubhuti-Kalita"* as Sri Sankara puts it in Viveka-Chudamani, Sloka 41.

स्वाश्रमं च स्वजातिं च स्वकीर्तिं पुष्टिवर्धनम् ।
एतत्सर्वं परित्यज्य गुरुमेव समाश्रयेत् ॥४१॥

41. Renouncing one's order of life, caste and growing reputation in society and other worldly attractions one should always depend on his Guru.

*Notes:* This applies to the whole-timed Sadhaka who renounces the world and takes shelter under the Guru.

The Sadhakas who are new to the spiritual path should definitely take advantage of the constant company and guidance of the Guru. Not properly guided by the Guru, the students are apt to go astray when Vairagya wanes, and Sadhana becomes dull.

अनन्याश्रितयन्तो ये सुलभं परमं सुखम् ।
तस्मात्सर्वप्रयत्नेन गुरोराराधनं कुरु ॥४२॥

42. Giving up entirely thoughts of the world and giving his exclusive attention and thought on the Guru, one attains the Supreme Bliss easily. Therefore, by every possible effort worship your Guru.

*Notes:* Worship of the Guru includes personal services rendered to him, living upon the ideals of the Guru, spreading the Upadesa (advices) of the Guru till the end of life. Not to do anything calculated to contradict the views and principles of the Guru is also worship of Guru.

गुरुवक्त्रे स्थिता विद्या गुरुभक्त्या च लभ्यते ।
त्रैलोक्ये स्फुटवक्तारो देवर्षिपितृमानवा: ॥४३॥

43. The disciples get, by devotion to the Guru, the knowledge which the Guru possesses. In the three worlds this fact is clearly enunciated by Divine sages, the Pitris (ancestors) and learned men.

*Notes:* History has recorded countless instances of disciples who have, by their devotion to their Guru, attained whatever they wanted. The four Purusharthas—Dharma, Artha, Kama and Moksha—wait upon the disciple of one-pointed devotion. The devotion of Ekalavya, Uttanka, Arjuna, Trotakacharya (the disciple of the world-famous Sri Sankaracharya, the exponent of Advaita Vedanta) is recorded in the pages of history. One need not at all doubt about the efficacy of Guru-Bhakti. There is no exaggeration also. Even in the present day we have heard of many instances of Guru-Bhakti succeeding and making the lives of the disciples brilliant and shining.

Getting a realised and Brahma Jnani Guru is on account of Isvara-Kripa and the student's own sincere devotion and qualifications. Devoted service done untiringly for a long number of years is required for the attainment of Guru-Kripa.

Guru-Kripa and Isvara-Kripa are interdependent. It is difficult to say which precedes. Saint Kabirdas once said, "Guru and Govinda both are before me. To whom shall I prostrate first? Certainly Guru is great because it is he who showed me the Lord. Only by his grace I get the vision of God Govinda." Thus the instances of the present-day-world, as also those described in the Vedas go to prove the importance of Guru-Bhakti.

गुकारश्चान्धकारो हि रुकारस्तेज उच्यते ।
अज्ञानग्रासकं ब्रह्म गुरुरेव न संशयः ॥४४॥

44. The letter 'Gu' denotes darkness, the letter 'Ru' denotes the remover of darkness. Brahman who is capable of swallowing up ignorance is certainly the Guru.

गुकारो भवरोगः स्यात् रुकारस्तन्निरोधकृत् ।
भवरोगहरत्वाच्च गुरुरित्यभिधीयते ॥४५॥

45. 'Gukara' means the disease of birth and death. 'Rukara' means the destroyer of births and deaths. On account of the power of destroying the disease of birth and death, the teacher is known by the significant name 'Guru'.

गुकारश्च गुणातीतो रूपातीतो रुकारकः ।
गुणरूपविहीनत्वात् गुरुरित्यभिधीयते ॥४६॥

46. The letter 'Gu' denotes that he is above the three Gunas and 'Ru' denotes that he is beyond forms. Because he is free from Gunas and forms he is called Guru.

गुकारः प्रथमो वर्णो मायादिगुणभासकः ।
रुकारोऽस्ति परं ब्रह्म मायाभ्रान्तिविमोचनम् ॥४७॥

47. The first syllable 'Gu' creates or makes manifest Maya and the Gunas. 'Ru' is Para Brahman that removes both Maya and delusion, viz., I am the body, I am the mind, etc.

एवं गुरुपदं श्रेष्ठं देवानामपि दुर्लभम् ।
गरुडोरगगन्धर्वसिद्धादिसुरपूजितम् ॥४८॥

48. Thus the state of the Guru (Gurupada) is great and sublime, very difficult for even Devas to attain and worthy of worship by Garuda, serpents, Gandharvas, Siddhas and the celestials.

ध्रुवं देवि मुमुक्षूणां नास्ति तत्त्वं गुरो: परम् ।
गुरोराराधानं कुर्यात् स्वजीवत्वं निवेदयेत् ।।४९।।

49. Guru Tattva is supreme. There is nothing greater than Guru. One should worship his Guru and dedicate himself—body, mind and soul—unto the Guru.

*Notes:* He should effect unconditioned self-surrender to the Guru so that he may be entitled to the highest knowledge of Brahman.

आसनं शयनं वस्त्रं वाहनं भूषणादिकम् ।
साधकेन प्रदातव्यं गुरुसन्तोषकारणम् ।।५०।।

50. The Sadhaka should present to the Guru seats, bedding, carriage, vehicles, ornaments, etc., conducive to his happiness.

*Notes:* The injunction contained in this verse is meant particularly for the householder disciples who can serve the Guru with such offerings. Verse 41 dealt with the duties of disciples who are whole-timed Sadhakas living with the Guru or who lead a renounced life.

कर्मणा मनसा वाचा सर्वदाऽऽराधयेद्गुरुम् ।
दीर्घदण्डं नमस्कृत्य निर्लज्जो गुरुसन्निधौ ।।५१।।

51. One should, in thought, word and deed, always worship the Guru with full prostrations placing the whole body flat in front of the Guru. He should never feel shy in doing such prostrations.

*Notes:* 'Dandavat' literally means that the disciple should fall flat like a stick let down. The disciple should be free from shyness of all sorts. He should be devoid of ego. He should prostrate thus in front of gods also. Some feel shy to do full prostrations. Such prostrations indicate that the disciple is free from egoism, that he is suppliant to the Guru and ready to carry out all his behests unselfishly and unreservedly.

शरीरमिन्द्रियं प्राणमर्थस्वजनबान्धवान् ।
आत्मदारादिकं सर्वं सद्गुरुभ्यो निवेदयेत् ॥५२

52. One should surrender himself completely to the Guru. The body, the senses, the Prana, wealth, one's own relations, the self, wife, etc.,—all these should be surrendered to the Guru.

*Notes:* He should surrender himself unreservedly. Not only the disciple but all his belongings, as detailed here, rightly belong to the Guru.

गुरुरेको जगत्सर्वं ब्रह्मविष्णुशिवात्मकम् ।
गुरोः परतरं नास्ति तस्मात्संपूजयेद्गुरुम् ॥५३

53. The entire creation consisting of Brahma, Vishnu and Siva is all Guru only. There is nothing greater than Guru. Therefore one should worship his Guru.

*Notes:* This is akin to the Brahmakara Vritti of the Vedantin who feels "All indeed is Brahman; there is nothing like duality—*Sarvam Brahmamayam Jagat Neha Nanasti Kinchana.*"

The Upanishad says, *"Drishtim Jnanamayeem Kritva Pasyet Brahmamayam Jagat*—possessing the Brahmic Vision one should see Brahman only everywhere."

Similarly, filled with the Guru-consciousness one should feel "everything is indeed Guru."

सर्वश्रुतिशिरो-रत्न-विराजित-पदाम्बुजम् ।
वेदान्तार्थप्रवक्तारं तस्मात् सम्पूजयेद्गुरुम् ॥५४॥

54. The holy lotus-like Feet of the Guru shine like the two pearls of the entire Srutis. He (Guru) is the exponent of the Truths of the Vedanta. Therefore one should worship his Guru.

*Notes:* A similar idea is found in the celebrated Sri Ramcharitamanas of Saint Tulasidasji, where he describes the Feet of the Guru as adorned with so many pearls shining as the finger-nails. He further says that the disciple who meditates on the light emanating from these pearls attains Divine Vision.

The verse is as follows:—

"Sri Guru Pada nakha mani gana jyoti;
Sumirat divya drishti hiya hoti."

यस्य स्मरणमात्रेण ज्ञानमुत्पद्यते स्वयम् ।
स एव सर्वसम्पत्तिः तस्मात्सम्पूजयेद्गुरुम् ॥५५॥

55. By the mere remembrance of whom knowledge (of Self) dawns in one automatically; he (the Guru) is one's entire wealth. Therefore, the aspirant should (ever) worship his Guru.

*Notes:* The life of the Guru is a constant source of inspiration for the student in the spiritual path. He gets inner spiritual strength to fight Maya. The disciple places before him the ideals of the Guru. He remembers the various incidents in his Guru's life and draws inspiration from him. Therefore, the real wealth for the disciple is his

Guru. That is the reason why so much stress is laid for Guru-Seva (the worship of the preceptor) in these verses.

"*Yasya Sravana-matrena*" is another version in place of "*Yasya Smarana-matrena*" with which the verse starts. In that case the verse would mean "the student attains knowledge by hearing the instructions of the Guru, etc." Sravana here means hearing of Vedantic Truths (Brahma Vidya) from the Guru.

कृमिकोटिभिराविष्टं दुर्गन्धकुलदूषितम् ।
अनित्यं दु:खनिलयं देहं विद्धि वरानने ॥५६॥

56. O Parvati, know this body as transitory, the abode of pains, full of worms, blood, faecal matter, urine and other foul-smelling things.

*Notes:* In the second half of the verse another version is seen as below. "*Sleshma-rakta-tvacha-mamsairnaddham chaitad-varanane.*" This makes practically no change in the sense conveyed by the verse.

The contents of the physical body are enumerated here to create dispassion in the minds of the Sadhakas. Lord Siva says to Parvati; but the advice goes to the students. He says, "O man! Have a good look at the contents of your physical body which you worship here with scents, soaps, silk, ornaments, etc." They are but tempting baits of Maya to dupe the Jivas bound in Samsara. The man of discrimination and dispassion does not fall a victim to it.

संसार-वृक्षमारूढा: पतन्ति नरकार्णवे ।
यस्तानुद्धरते सर्वान् तस्मै श्रीगुरवे नम: ॥५७॥

57. Those who have climbed the tree of Samsara fall

into the ocean of hell. Prostrations to that Guru who saves all such men from destruction.

*Notes:* The tree of Samsara grows by the side of the ocean of hell. The Jivas, who climb the Samsara-tree for shelter and enjoyment of the fruits thereof, soon find themselves helpless and tired and fall straight into the ocean of hell. This is the case of those who are without protection and help. But those people, who are protected by the Sadguru, fly to Moksha with the wings of Viveka and Vairagya. Thus they save themselves from falling a victim to messengers of hell.

गुरुर्ब्रह्मा गुरुर्विष्णुर्गुरुर्देवो महेश्वर: ।
गुरुरेव परं ब्रह्म तस्मै श्रीगुरवे नम: ॥५८॥

58. Guru is Brahma. Guru is Vishnu. Guru is God Mahesvara. Guru alone is verily the Supreme Brahman. Therefore prostrations to him (the Guru).

*Notes:* The first part of the second line of the verse is popularly read as *"Guruh Sakshat Param Brahma"* in place of *"Gurureva Param Brahma".* Guru is verily the perceptible concrete Supreme Reality.

The trinity of Brahma, Vishnu and Siva is Guru. So also the Brahman that transcends them. This verse establishes identity of the Guru with Brahman.

To the student, who has not seen the different parts of the globe, the teacher brings a toy globe wherein all countries are represented by lines and different colours. Even so, to the student, who has no realisation of Brahman, the Vedas have prescribed the Guru's form as representing Brahman. Brahma, Vishnu and Siva are superimposed on the Guru. This method of Sadhana is like the ladder kept on to reach the top branch of the tree with the help of which the person reaches the tree-top.

With the help of the Guru the student reaches Brahman, just as in idol-worship, the idol remains as idol but the worship reaches the Lord. Though you may not see immediately the result of such worship in the case of the Guru, the worship reaches the Ultimate represented by the Guru.

अज्ञानतिमिरान्धस्य ज्ञानांजनशलाकया ।
चक्षुरुन्मीलितं येन तस्मै श्रीगुरवे नमः ।।५९।।

59. I prostrate to that Guru who shows the supreme state of Brahman by the collyrium of knowledge to one who is blinded by the cataract of Ajnana (absence of knowledge).

*Notes:* The eye-specialist operates the eye affected by cataract and the patient is able to see things properly. Where there was intense darkness, now there is good light. So also, the teacher applies the collyrium of knowledge and the student gets the supreme vision and sees things clearly.

अखण्डमण्डलाकारं व्याप्तं येन चराचरम् ।
तत्पदं दर्शितं येन तस्मै श्रीगुरवे नमः ।।६०।।

60. I prostrate to the Sadguru by whom is the whole universe comprising of the unbroken consciousness pervaded and filled through and through in every moving and unmoving object, and who has brought to my intuitive vision the entire mass of supreme consciousness.

*Notes:* By this verse the names and extent of the different universes (Mandalas) are hinted. The different systems like the solar system, the stellar system are all pervaded by Brahman. The Guru reveals to the disciple all these and therefore he is superior to all.

स्थावरं जंगमं व्याप्तं यत्किंचित्सचराचरम् ।
त्वंपदं दर्शितं येन तस्मै श्रीगुरवे नमः ॥६१॥

61. Whatever is moving and unmoving here and that which pervades whatever is there with life and without life, to that Guru who reveals these and the real significance of TVAMPADA—be these prostrations.

चिन्मयं व्यापितं सर्वं त्रैलोक्यं सचराचरम् ।
असित्वं दर्शितं येन तस्मै श्रीगुरवे नमः ॥६२॥

62. I prostrate to that Guru who explains the Asi-Pada which pervades the three worlds as Chinmaya (mass of light) which moves and moves not.

*Notes:* Verses 60, 61 and 62 indicate that it is the Guru who illumines the disciple explaining the four Mahavakyas and points out to the disciple that he is Brahman by saying *"Tat Tvam Asi*—That thou art." With this knowledge the veil of ignorance that covers the student's understanding is rent asunder. There is no more ignorance and the Atman is realised.

निमिषान्निमिषार्धाद्वा यद्वाक्याद्वै विमुच्यते ।
स्वात्मानं शिवमालोक्य तस्मै श्रीगुरवे नमः ॥६३॥

63. Having perceived the Self, who is Siva, one frees himself (from the shackles of Maya) within a second or half-a-second by following the words of the Guru; prostrations be to that Guru.

चैतन्यं शाश्वतं शान्तं व्योमातीतं निरञ्जनम् ।
नादबिन्दुकलातीतं तस्मै श्रीगुरवे नमः ॥६४॥

64. Prostrations to that Guru who is eternal, peaceful,

unattached, full of light and knowledge, beyond the stages of Nada, Bindu and Kala and who transcends Akasa.

*Notes:* By saying that he transcends Akasa it is meant that he transcends all the five elements, earth, water, fire, air and ether. Akasa stands here for all the elements.

Nada, Bindu and Kala are the stages prior to creation of this universe. The meaning indicated here is that the Guru is beyond all these stages. The disciple, by Guru-kripa, is able to transcend the different stages and soar high in the realms of peace and bliss.

*"Nirmalam darsitam yena"* is another version in the second half of the verse.

निर्गुणं निर्मलं शान्तं जङ्गमं स्थिरमेव च ।
व्याप्तं येन जगत्सर्वं तस्मै श्रीगुरवे नमः ॥६५॥

65. That which is beyond the Gunas (Sattva, Rajas and Tamas), faultless, taintless, peaceful, moving and unmoving, that which pervades the whole world, that Sat-Guru, I worship.

स पिता स च मे माता स बन्धुः स च देवता ।
संसारमोहनाशाय तस्मै श्रीगुरवे नमः ॥६६॥

66. He is the father, he is the mother, he is the relative, and God to free us from the delusion of Samsara; therefore prostrations to Him.

यत्सत्त्वेन जगत्सत्यं यत्प्रकाशेन भाति यत् ।
यदानन्देन नन्दति तस्मै श्रीगुरवे नमः ॥६७॥

67. By whose potentiality this world appears to be

true, by whose light the world is illumined, by whose bliss all are happy here—to that Guru I prostrate.

यस्मिन् स्थितमिदं सर्वं भाति यद्भानरूपतः ।
प्रियं पुत्रादि यत्प्रीत्या तस्मै श्रीगुरवे नमः ॥६८॥

68. That in which this entire universe exists, by whose light everything is illumined here, by whose delight and love, son, etc., are dear to us, to that Guru I pay my homage.

*Notes:* The Sat, Chit, Ananda aspect in which everything is delighting in this world—that aspect is the Guru in reality.

येनेदं दर्शितं तत्त्वं चित्तचैत्यादिकं तथा ।
जाग्रत्स्वप्नसुषुप्त्यादि तस्मै श्रीगुरवे नमः ॥६९॥

69. By whose power we see everything here, by whose power the mind, intellect, Chitta, etc., function, by whose intelligence the different states of waking, dreaming and sleep are cognised, to that Guru I offer my worship.

यस्य ज्ञानमिदं विश्वं न दृश्यं भिन्नभेदतः ।
सदैकरूपरूपाय तस्मै श्रीगुरवे नमः ॥७०॥

70. Whose knowledge is this universe, in whom differences of sight and seen do not exist, who is ever established in the knowledge of oneness, to that Guru may these prostrations be.

*Notes:* There is nothing in this universe which is unknown to Him. But he himself is without difference of sight and seen. He always perceives oneness. He is established in his own Svarupa. Nothing affects him though acting in the world.

यस्य ज्ञातं मतं तस्य मतं यस्य न वेद स:
अनन्यभावभावाय तस्मै श्रीगुरवे नम: ॥७१॥

71. Brahman is really understood or properly understood by one who has realised that it ought to remain ever the unknown and the unknowable to him, but if one thinks he has known it, then, in fact, he does not know it at all. Therefore, one who is ever established in the One Bhava (knowledge) of the Self, to that Guru I ever prostrate.

This is a paraphrase of the Kena-Upanishad Mantra quoted below as *yasya amatam,* etc.

*Notes:* The first half of the verse indicates the knowledge of the Self. But the Guru is always established in that state of oneness with the Self. Therefore the disciple worships the Guru. The following is another version of the above verse.

"*Yadajnananmatam bhuyat na matam yasya vedanat;
Tadbrahma darsitam yena tasmai Sri Gurave namah.*"

In the Kena-upanishad there is an authoritative verse which deals with Brahman which is as follows:

"*Yasyamatam tasyamatam matam
yasya na veda saha;
Avijnatam vijanatam vijnatam avijanatam.*"

The meanings of both the verses are identical. One who says he knows Brahman, does not know. One who says he does not know, knows it. For, Brahman is not an object, but is always the subjective, Self, the Knower of Jnata. Such is the seeming contradiction in the knowledge of Self. He who knows both the known and the unknown is the Guru and so he is superior to all and is fit to be worshipped. Brahman is to be realised only as *Atma* or I or

*Aham*, Spirit or *Chit* or *Self* and not as matter or *Jneyam* or *Anatma* or *Idam*.

यस्मै कारणरूपाय कार्यरूपेण भाति यत् ।
कार्यकारणरूपाय तस्मै श्रीगुरवे नमः ॥७२॥

72. He who is the cause of all, yet appears to the world as the effect, my prostrations to Him who shares the nature of both cause and effect.

*Notes:* Brahman, though It is the cause of everything, appears to be the effect (the world).

नानारूपमिदं विश्वं न केनाप्यस्ति भिन्नता ।
कार्यकारणरूपाय तस्मै श्रीगुरवे नमः ॥७३॥

73. This world of diverse forms, in whom does not appear diversity, who shines as the cause and effect of everything—to that Guru I prostrate.

*Notes:* When the Atman is realised, diversity vanishes. The Jnani of Self-realisation sees no diversity anywhere. He feels and says like the great Self-realised Sage Sadasiva Brahman of Nerur (Trichy Dist., Tamil Nadu) *"Sarvam Brahmamayam Re Re Sarvam Brahmamayam*—Everything is Brahman O man, everything is Brahman". Where has the world of diversity disappeared which was appearing to me till now? asks the Jnani of realisation.

ज्ञानशक्तिसमारूढतत्त्वमालाविभूषिणे ।
भुक्तिमुक्तिप्रदात्रे च तस्मै श्रीगुरवे नमः ॥७४॥

74. He who is established in knowledge and power, who is adorned with the garland of Truth, the Reality, one who bestows both liberation and enjoyment here in this world, to that Guru, be this salutations.

# SRI GURU GITA

*Notes:* The sage of Self-realisation possesses all powers (Riddhis and Siddhis). They roll under his feet. He may not be even aware of them. He may not exhibit them. He can bestow everything the disciple wants. The disciples draw such powers and Siddhis to themselves from the Guru by their own faith, devotion and Sadhana.

अनेकजन्मसम्प्राप्तकर्मबन्धविदाहिने ।
ज्ञानानलप्रभावेन तस्मै श्रीगुरवे नमः ॥७५॥

75. He who breaks the bonds of Karma acquired in countless births by the power of the fire of knowledge, I prostrate to that Sri Guru.

*Notes:* By the fire of his Tapas, the Guru burns all Karmas of the student. The Bhagavad Gita says, *"Jnanagnih Sarvakarmani Bhasmasat Kurute Arjuna*—O Arjuna! The fire of knowledge burns all Karmas." Actually the Karmic bonds are burnt. This is the literal meaning.

शोषणं भवसिन्धोश्च दीपनं क्षरसंपदाम् ।
गुरोः पादोदकं यस्य तस्मै श्रीगुरवे नमः ॥७६॥

76. I prostrate to the Sadguru whose feet-washed-water has the power to dry up the ocean of Samsara and brighten one's position in life.

*Notes:* The literal meaning of *"Dipanam Kshara-Sampadam"* is that it brightens the wealth and possessions of the disciple—money, property and all prosperity of a worldly nature.

In the world, we have heard of fire burning wood, paper, cloth and all combustible things. Water wets. But the beauty of Guru-Kripa which works miracles, is that the water with which his feet are washed has the power to dry up the waters of the ocean of Samsara. Nowhere can any one prove of water having the power to dry up water. It can only make things wet or add to the existing quantity of water when added to any reservoir.

न गुरोरधिकं तत्त्वं न गुरोरधिकं तप: ।
न गुरोरधिकं ज्ञानं तस्मै श्रीगुरवे नम: ॥७७॥

77. There is no greater Truth than the Guru, no greater penance than the Guru, no knowledge greater than the Guru—therefore to that Guru I ever pay my homage.

मन्नाथ: श्रीजगन्नाथो मद्गुरु: श्री जगद्गुरु: ॥
ममात्मा सर्वभूतात्मा तस्मै श्रीगुरवे नम: ॥७८॥

78. My Lord is the Lord of the Universe, my Guru the world-Guru (guide for the entire world), my Self is the Self of all beings in this universe—therefore I prostrate to the Sadguru.

*Notes:* The knowledge of one's own Self being the Self of all is derived by the grace of the Guru. When the devotion to the Guru increases and becomes Ananya Prema this state is realised by the disciple.

गुरुरादिरनादिश्च गुरु: परमदैवतम् ।
गुरुमन्त्रसमो नास्ति तस्मै श्रीगुरवे नम: ॥७९॥

79. Guru is the foremost and the first. He is without a beginning. Guru is the Supreme Reality and deity. There is no Mantra equal to the Mantra of two syllables called "Guru" even as the one-syllabled Omkara is Brahman. Therefore prostrations to the Guru.

*Notes:* Refer to verse 151 said in the Guru-Gita. The faith that there is no Mantra equal to the Mantra imparted by Guru is very essential for Mantra Siddhi and realisation. Faith leads to perfect success and lack of faith is the cause of failure. He is the beginningless beginning and endless end reality where all worldly worries end. *Omityekaksharam Brahma Dvayakshram Gururuchyate.*

एक एव परो बन्धुर्विषमे समुपस्थिते ।
गुरु: सकलधर्मात्मा तस्मै श्रीगुरवे नम: ।।८०।।

80. There is one supreme help, relative and friend in this world when one is faced with adverse situations; Guru is the best Dharmatma, therefore prostrastions to the Guru.

*Notes:* Dharmatma means the knower and follower of all Dharma. The right interpretation of Dharma, the Guru gives. "Mahajano yena gatah sa panthah—the path is the one trodden by great men." The teachers tread the path themselves and set an example to others. The ways of Ativarnasramis and Yogis and Jivanmuktas are mysterious, beyond the reach of the ordinary man's intellect.

गुरुमध्ये स्थितं विश्वं विश्वमध्ये स्थितो गुरु: ।
गुरुर्विश्वं न चान्योऽस्ति तस्मै श्रीगुरवे नम: ।।८१।।

81. This universe is situated in the Guru and the Guru is in the midst of this world; this world itself is Guru (nothing else), therefore prostrations to the Guru.

*Notes:* The first-class student takes the world itself as the Guru. He sees his Guru everywhere. He sees all with Guru-buddhi. Just as the Jnani feels *"Sarvam Brahmamayam"*, the ideal disciples feel *"Sarvam Gurumayam"*.

भवारण्यप्रविष्टस्य दिङ्मोहभ्रान्तचेतस: ।
येन सन्दर्शित: पन्था: तस्मै श्रीगुरवे नम: ।।८२।।

82. To one confused in the forest of transmigration about the directions, etc., the one who shows the right path, to that Guru, be these salutations.

*Notes:* The transmigratory existence has been compared to a forest. A man entering a thick forest does not know which way to go. He misses even the directions, when the sun is not seen. Just as a person well-versed in the different directions in a forest can easily take the wandering traveller to his shelter and give him protection and assurance that he will save him and show the right path, so also in this forest of Samsara, Guru is the only guide for the man of the world. Without a guide the man lost in a forest goes from place to place and tires himself. Even so one without a Guru in the spiritual path wanders aimlessly and suffers the pangs of Samsara, birth, death, disease, family-afflictions, poverty, etc., etc.

तापत्रयाग्नितप्तानामशान्तप्राणिनां भुवि ।
यस्य पादोदकं गंगा तस्मै श्रीगुरुवे नमः ॥८३॥

83. Afflicted by the three kinds of fires, the restless creatures on earth wander aimlessly. To such people the feet-washed-water of the Guru is really Ganga. Prostrations to Him.

*Notes:* Adhyatmika, Adhibhautika, Adhidaivika are the three kinds of afflictions man is subjected to here. Adhyatmika Taapa is diseases of the body. Adhibhautika Taapa is afflictions inflicted by creatures like scorpion, snake, dog, etc. Adhidaivika Taapa is suffering caused by divine agencies like flood, thunder, lightning, heat, cold, earthquakes, etc.

*"Gurureva Para Ganga"* is another version of the first half of the second line. Guru is verily the supreme Ganga.

# SRI GURU GITA

अज्ञानसर्पदष्टानां प्राणिनां कश्चिकित्सक:
सम्यग्ज्ञानमहामन्त्रवेदिनं सद्गुरुं विना ॥८४॥

84. For those bitten by the cobra of ignorance there is no doctor other than the Guru who alone knows the Mahamantra of right knowledge (of the Self).

*Notes:* There is another version of the same verse in certain texts which is as follows:—

*Ajnanenahina grastah praninastan chikitsakah;*
*Vidyasvarupo bhagavan tasmai Sri Gurave namah.*

The meaning of this also is the same practically. In the second line there is a slight change as follows:

"One who is the form of knowledge and the Lord, to that Guru, I prostrate".

In the world we find that for a man bitten by a poisonous cobra, one who is well-versed in the Mantra Sastra is seen to be able to nullify the effect of poison by chanting the Garuda Mantra. The patient survives. This can be done only by the person who is well-versed in the Mantra and not by others. So also a *Srotriya* and *Brahmanishtha* Guru alone can save one from the ocean of *Samsara* and he is the Sadguru.

हेतवे जगतामेव संसारार्णवसेतवे ।
प्रभवे सर्वविद्यानां शंभवे गुरुवे नम: ॥८५॥

85. Prostrations to the Guru who is Sambhu, the cause of the world, the bridge to cross the ocean of Samsara and the source of all knowledge and sciences.

*Notes:* Bridging of the ocean is impossible. But the ocean of Samsara is bridged by the Guru. With the Guru, the impossible becomes possible.

ध्यानमूलं गुरोर्मूर्तिः पूजामूलं गुरोः पदम् ।
मन्त्रमूलं गुरोर्वाक्यं मुक्तिमूलं गुरोः कृपा ॥८६॥

86. The background (of thought) for meditation is the form of the Guru, the image for worship is the Guru's Feet, the sacred syllable (Mantra) for Japa is the words of the Guru and the cause of Moksha is the grace of Guru.

*Notes:* "Moksha mulam gurohkripa" this is a very popular alternative version of the last portion of this Sloka. The meaning is the same in both cases.

सप्तसागरपर्यन्तं तीर्थस्नानफलं तु यत् ।
गुरुपादपयोबिन्दोः सहस्रांशेन तत्फलम् ॥८७॥

87. Whatever merit is acquired from pilgrimages and bathing in the sacred waters extending to the seven seas by one, cannot be equal to even one thousandth part of the merit derived from partaking the feet-washed-water of the Guru.

*Notes:* The disciple whose faith is intense in his Guru, need not undertake tedious journeys and pilgrimages to the different rivers and oceans and other sacred waters prescribed by the scriptures. One drop of the Charanamrita of the Guru is enough to bestow on him all the merits acquired by such religious observances. Therefore what is wanted is faith, faith first and faith last.

शिवे रुष्टे गुरुस्त्राता गुरौ रुष्टे न कश्चन ।
लब्ध्वा कुलगुरुं सम्यग्गुरुमेव समाश्रयेत् ॥८८॥

88. When Siva is angry Guru can save you. If the Guru is angry nobody can save you. Therefore, having got the Kula Guru one should take refuge in him.

*Notes:* In the Ramacharitamanas there occurs a

story in the Uttarakand (towards the end), of a devotee who was devoted to Siva but showed lack of devotion to Guru when he came to the temple where he was practising his devotions. This attitude of the disciple roused anger in Lord Siva and He cursed the devotee. The Guru out of pity for his disciple pleaded with Lord Siva and got him freed from the curse with some ordinary punishment as Siva's anger cannot go in vain. This illustrates the importance of reverence to the Guru and why the student should avoid disregard to him.

Kula Guru means the family Guru. In the Ramayana we find that Vasishtha was the Kula Guru of the kings of the Raghu's Race. Even to Lord Rama Vasishtha was the Guru.

In the case of people having their Kula Guru it is advisable that they stick to them and honour their initiation.

Kula Guru is the same as Diksha Guru. For those who have a Kula Guru it is better for them to take Diksha from him. In the absence of such teachers one can take others in whom they have faith and devotion.

One who inspires you, in whom you have implicit faith and devotion, he is the Sadguru. If you have a Kula Guru and if your faith and devotion in him is implicit, you can take him as your Guru. That is the sense conveyed in this verse. This idea is further made clear in the following verse no. 89.

मधुलुब्धो यथा भृङ्गः पुष्पात् पुष्पान्तरं व्रजेत् ।
ज्ञानलुब्धस्तथा शिष्यो गुरोर्गुर्वन्तरं व्रजेत् ॥८९॥

89. Just as a bee thirsting for honey goes from one flower to another (till its thirst is satiated), so also the

disciple in quest of knowledge should approach different teachers.

*Notes:* The student should never be satisfied with the knowledge that he has attained. He must be ever in quest of knowledge. The method of Sadhana for realisation is pointed out by the Diksha Guru which should not be abandoned at any cost. The relationship between Guru and disciple is very sacred. The Diksha Guru should not be abandoned nor the Mantra given by him.

If a student thinks: "The Guru has not given the right initiation, let me approach another who will help me", it is lack of faith. This should not be the case. Mantra Sakti is hidden in the Mantra, Diksha awakens it and practice and devotion make you perfect.

The teacher who imparts knowledge of Sastra is Vidya Guru. Those who are conversant with the life of Lord Dattatreya and who have gone through Srimad Bhagavata know that he had not only one Guru. He collected knowledge just as the bee collects honey from different sources, and got convinced of what his Guru had taught him.

वन्दे गुरुपदद्वन्द्वं वाङ्मनोतीतगोचरम् ।
श्वेतरक्तप्रभाभिन्नं शिवशक्त्यात्मकं परम् ॥९०॥

90. I worship the two Feet of the Guru, endowed with the effulgence of Siva and Sakti Prabha, Supreme, differentiated by white and red colours, and which are beyond the reach of speech, mind and the senses.

*Notes:* In this verse there is a beautiful merging of the Guru Tattva and the Siva-Sakti Tattva. The fact that the Siva-Sakti Tattva and the Guru Tattva are identical is what is indicated in this verse.

This verse helps the meditation of the Sadhakas.

One, who can deeply reflect on the significance of this verse, can enter into deep meditation. The Siva-Sakti Tattva merges in the Guru Tattva.

गुकारं च गुणातीतं रुकारं रूपवर्जितम् ।
गुणातीतमरूपं च यो दद्यात् स गुरु: स्मृत: ।।९१।।

91. "Gu" indicates the state of the Guru who is above the three Gunas and "Ru" denotes freedom from the shackles of forms. One, who bestows the state beyond the three Gunas and the forms, is the Guru.

*Notes:* The Guru is capable of freeing the disciple from the three Gunas. He frees him from the illusion of names and forms also.

One who does this for you, he is the real Guru.

अत्रिनेत्र: शिव: साक्षात् द्विबाहुश्च हरि: स्मृत: ।
योऽचतुर्वदनो ब्रह्मा श्रीगुरु: कथित: प्रिये ।।९२।।

92. O Dear Parvati, Guru is Siva without three eyes. He is Hari with two hands. He is again Brahma without four faces.

*Notes:* Having two eyes Guru is Siva, with two hands he is really Hari and having only one face he is Brahma. Though the Guru does not possess these external symptoms of Brahma, Vishnu and Siva, he really represents them all to the disciple.

अयं मयाञ्जलिर्बद्धो दयासागरसिद्धये ।
यदनुग्रहतो जन्तुश्चित्रसंसारमुक्तिभाक् ।।९३।।

93. May these prostrations with folded hands be unto that ocean of mercy by whose grace beings get liberation from this multifarious Samsara.

*Notes:* The mention of Guru Kripa is very significant. Lord Siva is overpowered with feelings and He indirectly hints Guru Kripa without even mentioning the word Guru in this verse.

श्रीगुरो: परमं रूपं विवेकचक्षुरग्रत: ।
मंदभाग्या न पश्यन्ति अन्धा: सूर्योदयं यथा ॥९४॥

94. Just as the blind do not see the rising sun (or light), people of dull intellect and the unlucky do not see the Supreme Form of the Guru with the help of discrimination.

*Notes:* The man of dull intellect fails to behold the effulgent form of the Guru. What is meant here is that in the absence of a sharp and discriminative intellect a student cannot see the real form and glory of the Guru though he may have spent years or ages with him. Just as water does not penetrate stone even though it is put in water for a number of days, even so the student without the proper qualification cannot imbibe the teachings of the Guru even though he lives with him a long time. Grace of the Guru descends only on the best and qualified student. The students draw to themselves the grace of the Guru by their faith and devotion.

कुलानां कुलकोटीनां तारकस्तत्र तत्क्षणात् ।
अतस्तं सद्गुरुं ज्ञात्वा त्रिकालमभिवादयेत् ॥९५॥

95. Guru is the instantaneous saviour of one's family-line not only one but crores of generations. Knowing this, one should prostrate to the Sadguru thrice daily.

*Notes:* Just as to the Brahmana and the other two Varnas performance of Sandhya is compulsory and imperative, the worship of the Guru is prescribed for the disciple thrice daily. To the disciple, Guru represents all the deities and naturally performance of worship is directed to the Guru only in his case.

श्रीनाथचरणाद्वन्द्वं यस्यां दिशि विराजते ।
तस्यां दिशि नमस्कुर्याद् भक्त्या प्रतिदिनं प्रिये ॥९६॥

96. My dear Parvati! In whichever direction the holy Feet of Sri Natha (Sadguru) rest, to that place and direction prostrate with deep devotion everyday.

*Notes:* This applies to the disciple who stays far away from the Guru. When physical contact is not possible, then the disciple should reverently worship the Guru in the direction where he lives.

साष्टांगप्रणिपातेन स्तुवन्नित्यं गुरुं भजेत् ।
भजनात्स्थैर्यमाप्नोति स्वस्वरूपमयोभवेत् ॥९७॥

97. One should worship his Guru by daily performing full prostrations (Sashtanga Pranams) to him. By worship one attains steadiness and ultimately realises one's own true nature.

This is an outward expression of the inner Bhava of the disciple. When Bhava is lacking, the outer expressions also are absent. The inner feelings and devotion one has are expressed outwardly by the way one stands, moves and behaves in front of an elder.

Even the contents of the mind can be studied from the way one stands, one looks, one talks, etc. Even though one has not expressed anything, the contents of the mind can be known from the look. Face is the index of the mind and nothing is hidden from the eyes and the look.

दोभ्यां पद्भ्यां च जानुभ्यामुरसा शिरसा दृशा ।
मनसा वचसा चेति प्रणामोष्टांग उच्यते ॥९८॥

98. One should prostrate to the Guru fully lying flat on the ground with both hands, legs, knees, thighs, head, by sight, mind and speech. This kind of full prostration (where body, mind and senses are involved) is Sashtanga Pranama.

*Notes:* Though both hands, legs, knees and thighs are involved in the prostration, each pair is taken as one. Thus the four pairs really count only four.

Prostrating by mere show of hands or a smile or a simple bow of the head is not real prostration. Such prostration lacks the real inner Bhava and is not considered as proper prostration by the learned and the wise.

तस्यै दिशे सततमञ्जलिरेष नित्यं
प्रक्षिप्यतां मुखरितैर्मधुरैः प्रसूनैः ।
जागर्ति यत्र भगवान् गुरुचक्रवर्ती
विश्वस्थितिप्रलयनाटकनित्यसाक्षी ॥९९॥

99. To that direction where the Emperor Guru Bhagavan, the eternal witness of the Drama of the rise, stay and dissolution of this world, dwells, may this repeated worshipful offering of handfuls of fresh blooming flowers, be offered.

*Notes:* This verse gives a very high internal Bhava of the devotee or disciple who, in the absence of the Guru, is paying his homage to the great personality of the Guru by simply bowing to the direction where he lives or to his abode. Here, the Bhava is similar to that of the Gopis of Brindavan who had surrendered their body, mind and soul to Lord Krishna. They became Krishnamaya in a Tanmaya state of Krishna consciousness. The disciple becomes saturated with Guru Bhava and becomes Gurumaya.

अभ्यस्तै: किमु दीर्घकालविमलैर्व्याधिप्रदैर्दुष्करै:
प्राणायामशतैरनेककरणैर्दु:खात्मकैर्दुर्जयै: ।
यस्मिन्नभ्युदिते विनश्यति बली वायु: स्वयं तत्क्षणात्
प्राप्तं तत्सहजस्वभावमनिशं सेवेत चैकं गुरुम् ॥१००॥

100. Of what use is the hazardous, painful, long-drawn, doubtful practices, resulting in diseases, countless control of breath etc., when by the dawn of Guru's grace all difficulties in the path of Yoga vanish and the blissful state of that (coveted) Sahajavastha is attained. Therefore, one should worship and serve that Sadguru alone, the secondless One only.

*Notes:* While pointing out the hazardous nature of the different Yoga practices, the superiority and easily accomplishable method of Guru-Seva Yoga as the means to the attainment of Moksha or final beatitude is pointed out here. For, Guru-Seva is the only and easiest means to attain Sahaja-Avastha. To attain it, is just to understand that it is ever attained, as it is one's own natural state of being Sat-Chit-Ananda or Self, by Vidya or Guru's Upadesa or teaching only.

ज्ञानं विना मुक्तिपदं लभ्यते गुरुभक्तित: ।
गुरो: प्रसादतो नान्यत् साधनं गुरुमार्गिणाम् ॥१०१॥

101. By the devotion practised towards the Guru, one attains the state of Mukti even without knowledge. For those who tread the path of unflinching devotion to the

Guru, no other Sadhana is needed than the grace of the Guru (Guru Prasada).

*Notes:* In the second half of the verse in place of *"Prasadato"* there is another version *"Samanato"* which means "equal to".

To many this may sound very strange. The declaration of the Sruti is definite in that it says, *"Rite-jnanan na muktih"* without knowledge no one can attain Mukti. This verse wants to point out that the disciple, who is wholeheartedly devoted to the Guru and who is unmindful of anything other than Guru-Seva, attains knowledge by the grace of the Guru. In other words, his devotion to the Guru automatically draws knowledge to him without any effort.

In the Chhandogya Upanishad you will find the story of Satyakama Jabala and Upakoshala. Here the Agni Deva pleased with the devoted service of the disciple Upakoshala initiates him into the knowledge of Brahman. When he returns to the Ashram, the Guru sees the disciple shining with Brahmic splendour. The Guru questions the disciple—"You are now shining with Brahmic splendour. Tell me truly, who has instructed you into Brahma Vidya?" To this Upakoshala says, "O Lord! Agni Deva taught me the knowledge of Brahman finding me fit for it." In this case Guru-Seva has given him knowledge. The instructions by Agni Deva is nothing but Guru-Kripa.

यस्मात्परतरं नास्ति नेति नेतीति वै श्रुति: ।
मनसा वचसा चैव सत्यमाराधयेद्गुरुम् ॥१०२॥

102. The Srutis declare "Neti, Neti—not this, not this", and speak of something beyond which there is nothing—that Tattva is the Guru in reality. One should,

therefore, through the (Trikarana) mind, speech and actions worship the Guru.

गुरो: कृपाप्रसादेन ब्रह्माविष्णुशिवादय:
सामर्थ्यमभजन् सर्वे सृष्टिस्थित्यन्तकर्मणि ॥१०३॥

103. It is by the grace of the Guru that Brahma, Vishnu and Siva became capable of performing their respective duties—creation, preservation and dissolution. Therefore, one should always worship the Guru.

*Notes:* By showing that the supreme cause, the controller and destroyer of the world is Guru, this verse declares the identity of Guru and Brahman.

देवकिन्नरगन्धर्वा: पितृयक्षास्तु तुम्बरु: ।
मुनयोऽपि न जानन्ति गुरुशुश्रूषणे विधिम् ॥१०४॥

104. Even the Devas, the Kinnaras, Gandharvas, Pitris, Yakshas and sages like Tumburu and others do not know the right technique of service to the Guru.

*Notes:* Service of Guru is very difficult. The disciple may serve the Guru in his own way by adopting such methods that he thinks will please the Guru. In reality the Guru may not be pleased. The whole technique of Guru-Seva lies in knowing the heart of the Guru, the taste, the temperament, etc., of the Guru and serving him in a way that pleases him.

The descent of knowledge of Brahman in a disciple indicates that he has achieved Guru-Kripa. All services are therefore only preparatory to knowledge and Guru-Kripa.

Absence of egoism together with all traces thereof is the qualification for Guru-Kripa. The above named gods and celestial beings are not free from egoism and so they cannot know what real Guru-Seva is.

तार्किकाश्छान्दसाश्चैव दैवज्ञाः कर्मठाः प्रिये ।
लौकिकास्ते न जानन्ति गुरुतत्त्वं निराकुलम् ॥१०५॥

105. People who are well-versed in Tarkasastra, in the Vedic Chhandas, knowers of divine beings like gods, Karmakandins, people versed in worldly sciences—none of them knows the Guru-Tattva in its entirety.

*Notes:* The thoughts given here are in continuation of the expressions contained in the previous verse. This verse deals with Guru-Tattva and its importance. The previous one stressed the importance of Guru-Seva.

The ideal and goal of those persons mentioned here are not cent-per-cent spiritual. They lay stress on different sciences. But those who are endowed with Viveka and Vairagya and who strive hard to attain liberation, really seek the knowledge of Brahman, and the guidance of the teacher (Guru) is indispensable for them. So, it is really the Sadhakas who know Guru-Tattva better than others mentioned here.

महाहंकारगर्वेण तपोविद्याबलेन च ।
भ्रमन्त्येतस्मिन् संसारे घटीयन्त्रं यथा पुनः ॥१०६॥

106. On account of great egoism, pride, power of Tapas and education, (people) roam about in this world like the pots in a Persian wheel.

*Notes:* The Persian wheel is a very apt example for the wheel of Samsara. Moved by pride and egoism everyone here engages himself in some work or other which is creative of bondage and the wheel of birth and death goes on moving. Caught helplessly in this wheel, beings move here.

यज्ञिनोऽपि न मुक्ता: स्यु: न मुक्ता योगिनस्तथा ।
तापसा अपि नो मुक्ता गुरुतत्त्वात्पराङ्मुखा: ॥१०७॥

107. Neither those who perform great sacrifices, nor Yogis, nor those who practise severe austerities are liberated without the true knowledge of Guru-Tattva.

*Notes:* It is indicated here that no one who is not devoted to the Guru can attain knowledge of the Self, even though he my be an expert in Yoga or a Tapasvi who can mortify his body with hard penances, etc., or a Karmakandi or an expert in Mantra and Tantra Sastras and sacrifices.

न मुक्तास्तु गन्धर्वा: पितृयक्षास्तु चारणा: ।
ऋषय: सिद्धदेवाद्या: गुरुसेवापराङ्मुखा: ॥१०८॥

108. Those, who are averse to the service of the preceptor, cannot expect to be liberated from the cycle of Samsara (birth and death), even if they are Gandharvas, Pitris, Yakshas, Charanas, Rishis, Siddhas or Devas.

इति श्रीस्कान्दोत्तरखण्डे सनत्कुमारसंहितायां
उमामहेश्वरसंवादे श्रीगुरुगीतायां प्रथमोऽध्याय: ॥

Thus ends the first chapter of the Guru Gita, being a dialogue between Sri Uma and Sri Mahesvara (Parvati and Siva), which forms a part of the Sanat Kumara Samhita, in the Uttarakhanda of the Skanda Purana.

## CHAPTER II

ध्यानं शृणु महादेवि सर्वानन्दप्रदायकम् ।
सर्वसौख्यकरं चैव भुक्तिमुक्तिप्रदायकम् ॥१०९॥

109. O Mahadevi, hear Thou the method of meditation (on the Guru), the bestower of all bliss, joy and happiness. It is the giver of all Bhukti and Mukti and all kinds of happiness.

*Notes:* Commencing from this verse till the 125th verse the method of meditation on the Guru is prescribed. Aspirants may choose any method suitable to them. A combination of the different methods also can be done if found suitable.

Bhukti is worldly prosperity and happiness. Mukti is emancipation from the cycle of birth and death.

श्रीमत्परं ब्रह्म गुरुं स्मरामि
श्रीमत्परं ब्रह्म गुरुं भजामि ।
श्रीमत्परं ब्रह्म गुरुं वदामि
श्रीमत्परं ब्रह्म गुरुं नमामि ॥११०॥

110. I meditate on the Sadguru, I pray to the Sadguru who is himself Parabrahman, I speak of the Sadguru and I prostrate to the Sadguru.

*Notes:* The different mental and physical acts are directed to the Guru. Meditate on the form of the Guru. Worship the Guru as you do the Lord with the 16 kinds of Upacharas (formalities). Speak of the Guru to devotees and disciples around; about his life and teachings.

Physically prostrate in the *Sashtanga* way described in verse 97 wherein all the parts of the body lie flat on the ground, the hands touching the Feet of the Guru. The right hand should touch the right leg and the left hand should touch the left leg.

These can be done both physically and mentally. During meditation one should do only mentally because one may or may not sit in front of the Guru during one's meditation.

ब्रह्मानन्दं परमसुखदं केवलं ज्ञानमूर्तिं
द्वन्द्वातीतं गगनसदृशं तत्त्वमस्यादिलक्ष्यम् ।
एकं नित्यं विमलमचलं सर्वधीसाक्षिभूतं
भावातीतं त्रिगुणरहितं सद्गुरुं तं नमामि ।।१११।।

111. I adore the Sadguru, the bestower of supreme happiness, the bliss of Brahman, who is Knowledge Absolute, the one without a second, who is beyond the pairs of opposites, expansive and pervasive like the sky, the goal indicated by the Mahavakya *Tattvamasi*, the one eternal, pure, unchanging, the witness of all functions of the intellect, who is above all Bhavas (mental conditions) and the three Gunas (Sattva, Rajas and Tamas).

*Notes:* This is an all-inclusive prayer covering almost all aspects of the Nirguna Brahman. A proper understanding of the truths contained here is enough to put one in a blissful state. As such, this is very suitable and this is most popular among all Sadhakas. The Sadhaka who wishes to meditate may rotate his mind on the various ideas contained here one by one and fix his mind on the best idea for a long time to enjoy the best meditation for a long time.

हृदंबुजे कर्णिकमध्यसंस्थे
सिंहासने संस्थितदिव्यमूर्तिम् ।
ध्यायेद्गुरुं चन्द्रकलाप्रकाशं
सच्चित्सुखाभीष्टवरं दधानम् ॥११२॥

112. The disciple should meditate on the Guru as seated on the Divine throne in the Lotus of the heart. He should meditate on the Divine form of the Guru emanating light as though from the full moon. It is capable of bestowing on the meditator the boon of the bliss of Sat (existence), Chit (light) and wished boons.

*Notes:* When the thoughts of the meditator dwell on the different aspects and beautiful forms suggested, he will enjoy supreme joy and happiness. They are capable of driving away worldly thoughts and distractions.

श्वेताम्बरं श्वेतविलेपपुष्पं
मुक्ताविभूषं मुदितं द्विनेत्रम् ।
वामाङ्कपीठस्थितदिव्यशक्तिं
मन्दस्मितं पूर्णकृपानिधानम् ॥११३॥

ज्ञानस्वरूपं निजभावयुक्तम्
आनन्दमानन्दकरं प्रसन्नम् ।
योगीन्द्रमीड्यं भवरोगवैद्यं
श्रीमद्गुरुं नित्यमहं नमामि ॥११४॥

113 & 114. I always prostrate to the Sri Sadguru who is the Yogindra, fit to be worshipped, the doctor who cures the disease of birth and death, who is ever blissful, who being himself bliss distributes bliss to all, who is ever cheerful, full of knowledge, endowed with the knowledge of Self, wearing white apparel, bedecked with white

# SRI GURU GITA

flowers, to whose left side is seated the Divine Sakti, who is with cheerful countenance, who bestows on all full Kripa-Kataksha (kindly-look), and who has two eyes.

वन्दे गुरुणां चरणारविन्दं
संदर्शितस्वात्मसुखांबुधीनाम् ।
जनस्य येषा गुलिकायमानं
संसारहालाहलमोहशान्त्यै ॥११५॥

115. I adore the Lotus-Feet of the teachers who have shown to us the source of the eternal ocean of bliss, born of the Self within, who have given us the remedy for the Halahala poison of Samsara.

*Notes*: Here worship is offered to all teachers collectively. The entire Guru Parampara (the line of Gurus) is worshipped.

Halahala is the deadliest poison that emanated from the mouth of the snake Vasuki at the time of the churning of the milky ocean by the Devas and the demons. The story of Amrita Mathana occurs in the Srimad Bhagavata.

यस्मिन् सृष्टिस्थितिध्वंसनिग्रहानुग्रहात्मकम् ।
कृत्यं पंचविधं शश्वत् भासते तं गुरुं भजेत् ॥११६॥

116. One should worship that Guru in whom the five kinds of grace are ever present, viz., creation, maintenance, destruction, Nigraha (punishment) and Anugraha (blessing).

*Notes*: The disciple has to superimpose the Divine qualities of the Lord on his own Guru. The powers enumerated here belong to the Lord. As pointed out a number of times in the first chapter, the importance of the Guru in the eye of the disciple should be great and he should view him as such so that he may be able to draw grace and power from his Guru, who is for all outward appearance a human being like others.

पादाब्जे सर्वसंसारदावकालानलं स्वके ।
ब्रह्मरन्ध्रे स्थिताम्भोजमध्यस्थं चन्द्रमण्डलम् ॥११७॥

117. The Guru in his holy lotus-like-Feet possesses the forest-fire needed to burn the entire Samsara forest (of the disciple) and has got in crown of his head (Brahma Randhra) the moon-like nectar which is capable of destroying the flames of Samsara and bestowing immortality on the disciple.

*Notes*: The idea contained in this verse is complete only in the next verse and as such the verb is seen in the next verse. The idea in this verse is given a complete touch here by adding suitable verbs.

अकथादित्रिरेखाब्जे सहस्रदलमण्डले ।
हंसपार्श्वत्रिकोणे च स्मरेत्तन्मध्यगं गुरुम् ॥११८॥

118. One should meditate on the Guru seated in the thousand-petalled lotus of the three Mandala triangle where the three lines (of the triangle) describe the Akara, Kakara and Thakara.

*Notes*: The secrets of the Mandalas and other details of the triangle where the different letters consisting of vowels and consonants of the alphabet are described in detail in authoritative books like Mantramahodadhi dealing with the entire range of Mantra Sastras. A mere hint is given here. Details can be had in the authoritative Mantra Sastras of which Mantramahodadhi is the prominent one.

नित्यं शुद्धं निराभासं निराकारं निरञ्जनम् ।
नित्यबोधं चिदानन्दं गुरुं ब्रह्म नमाम्यहम् ।।११९।।

119. That eternally pure, formless, unattached, unmanifested, constant knowledge of the Eternity, Knowledge-Bliss—to that Guru, I always offer my prostrations.

सकलभुवनसृष्टि: कल्पिताशेषसृष्टि-
निखिलनिगमदृष्टि: सत्पदार्थैकसृष्टि: ।
अतद्गुणपरमेष्टि: सत्पदार्थैकदृष्टि:
भवगुणपरमेष्टिर्मोक्षमार्गैकदृष्टि: ।।१२०।।

सकलभुवनरंगस्थापनास्तम्भयष्टि:
सकरुणरसवृष्टिस्तत्त्वमालासमष्टि: ।
सकलसमयसृष्टिस्सच्चिदानन्ददृष्टि:
निवसतु मयि नित्यं श्रीगुरोर्दिव्यदृष्टि: ।।१२१।।

120. & 121. May the Divine Vision of the Sadguru ever dwell in me. The Divya Drishti of the Guru is so powerful that on it depends the entire world creation, on whom all this creation is superimposed (seems to exist), on whom depend the entire Vedic injunctions and knowledge, in whom rests the entire creation, on whom depend the ways of Brahma and his creation, of Samsara (comprising of appearance and disappearance), in whom rests the one path to liberation, the support of creation comprising of so many worlds, the rain of whose merciful glance bestows the knowledge of Self, the vision of Satchidananda and all creative existences.

न गुरोरधिकं न गुरोरधिकं
न गुरोरधिकं न गुरोरधिकम् ।
शिवशासनतः शिवशासनतः
शिवशासनतः शिवशासनतः ॥१२२॥

122. There is nothing greater than Guru, there is nothing greater than Guru, there is nothing greater than Guru, nothing greater than Guru. By the command of Siva (I say this), by the command of Siva (I say this), by the command of Siva (I say this), by the command of Siva (I emphasise this).

*Notes:* In this and the two verses that follow, the repetitions show the firm conviction that the preceptor alone is everything and the disciple should be fully aware of this truth. The authority of Brahma, Vishnu and Siva is given to remove all doubts from the disciple's mind.

When there is doubt in the mind of the aspirant about the truth of a particular thing, he cannot have the right conviction. By repeated assertions all doubts are cleared.

इदमेव शिवं इदमेव शिवं
इदमेव शिवं इदमेव शिवम् ।
हरिशासनतो हरिशासनतो
हरिशासनतो हरिशासनतः ॥१२३॥

123. By the authority of Vishnu this alone is Siva (auspicious). By the authority of Vishnu this alone is Siva. By the authority of Vishnu this alone is Siva. By the authority of Vishnu this alone is Siva.

विदितं विदितं विदितं विदितं
विजनं विजनं विजनं विजनम् ।

विधिशासनतो विधिशासनतो
विधिशासनतो विधिशासनत: ॥१२४॥

124. By the order of Brahma this is the singular, unchallengeable Truth. By the authority of Brahma this is the singular, unchallengeable truth. By the order of Brahma this is the one Truth. By the command of Brahma this is the real Truth.

एवं विधं गुरुं ध्यात्वा ज्ञानमुत्पद्यते स्वयम् ।
तदा गुरुपदेशेन मुक्तोऽहमिति भावयेत् ॥१२५॥

125. Thus meditating on the Guru one acquires real knowledge. One should then strongly feel: "By the instructions of the Guru I am liberated."

*Notes:* This kind of meditation leads to Mukti. The injunction to meditate on the Guru and repetition of the formula *"Muktoham"* is the same as the Guru's instructions conveyed in the *Mahavakyas "Tattvamasi"*, etc., and the consequent realisation: "I am Brahman—*Aham Brahmasmi"*. The Guru says *"Tattvamasi"* and the disciple asserts and feels ,*"Aham Brahmasmi"*. This is *Anubhava Vakya* among the four *Mahavakyas*.

गुरुपदिष्टमार्गेण मनःशुद्धिं तु कारयेत् ।
अनित्यं खण्डयेत् सर्वं यत्किंचिदात्मगोचरम् ॥१२६॥

126. One should purify his mind by the method prescribed by the teacher. With the knowledge of the Self (Atman) one should reject everything else as unreal.

*Notes*: The means for purifying the mind should be given to the disciple by the Guru. The disciple needs the help of the Guru at all times and particularly so in the method of purifying the mind. Only one who has tread the path of Sannyasa and who has purified his own mind, can help another in doing so. The guide should himself first know the path and then only he can guide others.

If even after the instructions of the Guru regarding the knowledge of the Self, the disciple finds difficulty in rejecting the transitory things, he should with the help of the knowledge of Self (as advised by the Guru) reject all unreal objects and identify himself with the Atman. The unreal will persist till the dawn of knowledge of Self (Atma Sakshatkara).

ज्ञेयं सर्वं प्रतीतं च ज्ञानं च मन उच्यते ।
ज्ञानं ज्ञेयं समं कुर्यान्नान्य: पन्था द्वितीयक: ।।१२७।।

127. All things that pass off for knowledge, all appearances, objects of knowledge all these come within the realm of mind. Knowledge and the known should be on an equal footing. There is no other way (for the attainment of knowledge).

*Notes*: The meaning is "Self is the only reality. All else is illusory."

किमत्र बहुनोक्तेन शास्त्रकोटिशतैरपि ।
दुर्लभा चित्तविश्रान्ति: विना गुरुकृपां पराम् ।।१२८।।

128. Of what use is too much dilation by crores of thousands of scriptures even? Real peace of the Chitta (mind) is very rare. How can it be attained without Guru Kripa?

करुणाखड्गपातेन छित्वा पाशाष्टकं शिशो: ।
सम्यगानन्दजनक: सद्गुरु: सोऽभिधीयते ।।१२९।।

129. He is the Sadguru responsible for the rise of the

# SRI GURU GITA

knowledge of Self, who cuts asunder, for the disciple, the eight kinds of attachment by the sword of mercy (Karuna).

*Notes*: Doubts, pity, fear, shyness, censure, position in society, high birth and wealth are the eight kinds of attachment.

एवं श्रुत्वा महादेवि गुरुनिन्दां करोति यः ।
स याति नरकान् घोरान् यावच्चन्द्रदिवाकरौ ॥१३०॥

130. Having heard (the importance of the Guru), O Mahadevi, whoever indulges in vilifying the teacher goes to terrible hells and stays there as long as the sun and moon shine on earth.

यावत्कल्पान्तको देहस्तावद्देवि गुरुं स्मरेत् ।
गुरुलोपा न कर्तव्यः स्वच्छन्दो यदि वा भवेत् ॥१३१॥

131. O Devi, one should think of his Guru, as long as he has a body, may be till the end of a Kalpa (world cycle of creation). Neglect of the Guru should never be done even if one becomes independent, a free bird.

हुंकारेण च वक्तव्यं प्राज्ञशिष्यै: कदाचन ।
गुरोरग्रे न वक्तव्यमसत्यं तु कदाचन ॥१३२॥

132. The intelligent disciple should never slight his Guru. One should never utter falsehood in the presence of the Guru.

*Notes*: The utterance of the word "Hum" denotes contempt. Such words should never be used in front of the Guru.

गुरुं त्वंकृत्य हुंकृत्य गुरुसान्निध्यभाषणः ।
अरण्ये निर्जले देशे सम्भवेद् ब्रह्मराक्षसः ॥१३३॥

133. To speak in front of the Guru with disrespect by using "hum" and "tvam" (addressing the Guru in singular number as though to an inferior or equal) is a great sin. Such a person will become a Brahma-Rakshasa in a forest or waterless place (desert).

*Notes:* Brahma-Rakshasa is a species of devils.

अद्वैतं भावयेन्नित्यं सर्वावस्थासु सर्वदा ।
कदाचिदपि नो कुर्यादद्वैतं गुरुसन्निधौ ॥१३४॥

134. At all times and under all conditions feel the non-duality of the Self as "Brahman alone exists, I am Brahman". But never, in the presence of the Guru, should you have this Bhava (feeling).

*Notes:* One should never fail to pay due respects to the Guru when he comes, however much may be the height of one's realisation.

दृश्यविस्मृतिपर्यन्तं कुर्याद् गुरुपदार्चनम् ।
तादृशस्यैव कैवल्यं न च तद्व्यतिरेकिण: ॥१३५॥

135. One should worship the Feet of the Sadguru till the 'seen' disappears (absence of duality). To those only there is liberation and not to those who act in contradiction.

*Notes*: Until one merges in the Parabrahman, one should be devoted to the Guru by the Trikaranas (mind, body and speech). This is the import of this verse. The spirit of service should never be ignored.

अपि सम्पूर्णतत्त्वज्ञो गुरुत्यागी भवेद्यदा ।
भवत्येव हि तस्यान्तकाले विक्षेपमुत्कटम् ॥१३६॥

136. Even though one is a knower of the entire truth

(knower of all Sastras), if he is a Guru-Tyagi (abandoner of the teacher), he will face, at the time of death, great distraction.

गुरुकार्यं न लंघेत नापृष्ट्वा कार्यमाचरेत् ।
न ह्युत्तिष्ठेद्दिशेऽनत्वा गुरुसद्भावशोभितः ॥१३७॥

137. One should never ignore duties towards the Guru. One should do nothing without consulting him. One should not get up without prostrating to the Guru. These are the characteristics of one who is keenly devoted to the Guru (who shines in Gurubhava).

गुरौ सति स्वयं देवि परेषां तु कदाचन ।
उपदेशं न वै कुर्यात् तथा चेद्राक्षसो भवेत् ॥१३८॥

138. When the Guru is himself present, one should never give instructions to others. If he does so, he becomes a demon.

न गुरोराश्रमे कुर्यात् दुष्पानं परिसर्पणम् ।
दीक्षा व्याख्या प्रभुत्वादि गुरोराज्ञां न कारयेत् ॥१३९॥

139. In the Guru's Ashram one should avoid indulgence in waste of time by drinking liquors or such acts (prohibited for disciples). One should never put on a lordly show before the Guru, or indulge in tall talks, lectures showing one's own greatness, or initiation of disciples, etc.

नोपाश्रमं च पर्यमं न च पादप्रसारणम् ।
नांगभोगादिकं कुर्यान्न लीलामपरामपि ॥१४०॥

140. Sitting very close, using luxuries like cushions,

stretching of the legs, shampooing and other luxuries should never be indulged in the presence of the teacher.

गुरुणां सदसद्वापि तदुक्तं तन्न लंघयेत् ।
कुर्वन्नाज्ञां दिवा रात्रौ दासवन्निवसेद्गुरौ ॥१४१॥

141. One should never ignore the orders of the Guru, be it just or unjust. Carrying out his behests, one should live, day and night like a servant, with the Guru.

अदत्तं न गुरोर्द्रव्यमुपभुञ्जीत कर्हिचित् ।
दत्ते च रंकवद्ग्राह्यं प्राणोऽप्येतेन लभ्यते ॥१४२॥

142. One should never enjoy the wealth not given by the Guru. Those which are given by him, one should enjoy like a servant. One attains thereby great merit and longevity.

पादुकासनशय्यादि गुरुणा यदभीष्टितम् ।
नमस्कुर्वीत तत्सर्वं पादाभ्यां न स्पृशेत् क्वचित् ॥१४३॥

143. Shoes, sandals, seats, beds, etc., used by the Guru should never be touched by one's feet. On the other hand he should prostrate to the articles also (being sacred).

गच्छत: पृष्ठतो गच्छेत् गुरुच्छायां न लंघयेत् ।
नोल्बणं धारयेद्वेषं नालंकारांस्ततोल्बणान् ॥१४४॥

144. While the Guru walks the disciple should follow him. He should never cross the Guru's shadow. He should not imitate the Guru's dress, ornaments, etc. (No actions of the Guru should be imitated by the disciple nor should he pose himself like the Guru).

गुरुनिन्दाकरं दृष्ट्वा धावयेदथ वासयेत् ।
स्थानं वा तत्परित्याज्यं जिह्वाछेदाक्षमो यदि ॥१४५॥

145. One should leave the presence of the person speaking ill of the preceptor immediately (for a temporary period or permanently even), if he cannot cut his tongue.

*Notes*: One remaining in the presence of a person who insults his Guru, tolerates the insult, shares the sin of the person insulting the Guru. A true disciple should close his ears and run away from the presence of the insulter.

नोच्छिष्टं कस्यचिद्देयं गुरोराज्ञां न च त्यजेत् ।
कृत्स्नमुच्छिष्टमादाय हविर्वद्भक्षयेत् स्वयम् ॥१४६॥

146. One should never disregard the orders of his Guru. He should not share with others the leavings of the food-plate of the Guru. Taking the entire Ucchishta (leavings) one should eat the whole share taking it to be the leavings of a great sacrifice.

नानृतं नाप्रियं चैव न गर्वं नापि वा बहु ।
न नियोगधरं ब्रूयात् गुरोराज्ञां विभावयेत् ॥१४७॥

147. Do not utter falsehood to the teacher nor what is displeasing to him. Speak not with pride. Speak not too much in front of the Guru. Do not speak in a commanding tone to the Guru. Carry out implicitly the orders of the Guru.

प्रभो देवकुलेशानां स्वामिन् राजन् कुलेश्वर ।
इति सम्बोधनैर्भीतो सञ्चरेद्गुरुसन्निधौ ॥१४८॥

148. O Lord, O God, O best among men, O king,—thus one should address the Guru with devotion,

respect and awe. He should behave with respect and fear in front of the Guru.

*Notes*: The last portion has another version in the verse which reads as follows—*"Guru Bhavena Sarvada"*— meaning that one should always address the Guru with the feeling and Bhava (regard) that he is a Guru.

मुनिभि: पन्नगैर्वापि सुरैर्वा शापितो यदि ।
कालमृत्युभयाद्वापि गुरु: सत्राति पार्वति ॥१४९॥

149. Even though cursed by saints, gods or faced by danger from serpents, from death (Kala), Guru becomes the Saviour, O Parvati.

अशक्ता हि सुराद्याश्च ह्यशक्ता मुनयस्तथा ।
गुरुशापोपपन्नस्य रक्षणाय च कुत्रचित् ॥१५०॥

150. Even gods and sages are helpless to save one who is faced with the curse of the Guru.

*Notes*: Under no circumstances one should incur the displeasure of the Guru.

मन्त्रराजमिदं देवि गुरुरित्यक्षरद्वयम् ।
स्मृतिवेदपुराणानां सारमेव न संशय: ॥१५१॥

151. The two-lettered word "Guru", O Devi, (Lord Siva says to Parvati) is the king among Mantras. It is the essence of the Vedas, Smritis and Puranas.

सत्कारमानपूजार्थं दण्डकाषायधारण: ।
स संन्यासी न वक्तव्य: संन्यासी ज्ञानतत्पर: ॥१५२॥

152. One who wears the ochre-coloured robes and

the Danda (staff) for the sake of honour, respect and worship cannot be called a Sannyasin. A Sannyasin is one who is intent on the knowledge of the Self.

*Notes*: There is another version of the same verse with the first half of the first line remaining the same. The changed portion reads, *"...Gurusabda-dharo narah; Sa yati narakan Devi nasti sandehamanvapi."* It means that one, who calls himself a Guru for the sake of worship, respect, etc., goes to hell. There is no doubt in this.

This is pure exploitation of the innocent and ignorant. No sincere man should take to this. In so doing, he is open to scandal here in this world and the threat of hell after death.

विजानन्ति महावाक्यं गुरोश्चरणसेवया ।
ते वै संन्यासिन: प्रोक्ता इतरे वेषधारिण: ॥१५३॥

153. They who understand the significance of the Mahavakyas by the service of the Guru, are real Sannyasins. The others are mere wearers of the ochre-coloured dress.

नित्यं ब्रह्म निराकारं निर्गुणं सत्यचिद्घनम् ।
य: साक्षात्कुरुते लोके गुरुत्वं तस्य शोभते ॥१५४॥

154. Whoever realises here the Eternal Brahman that is Truth, knowledge Absolute, attributeless and formless, his teachership shines here in this world.

*Notes*: *"Nityam brahma nirakaram nirgunam bodhayet param; Bhasayan brahmabhavam cha dipo dipantaram yatha,"* is another version of the same verse which means that should one realise the True Brahman, attributeless and perfect, one shines in his own glory like the light that shines brilliantly without the help of any other.

गुरुप्रसादत: स्वात्मन्यात्मारामनिरीक्षणात् ।
समता मुक्तिमार्गेण स्वात्मज्ञानं प्रवर्तते ॥१५५॥

155. By steadiness in the path to Mukti, by seeing one's own Self in oneself, by the practice of introspection within and by the grace of the Guru, the knowledge of the Self dawns in the Sadhaka.

आब्रह्मस्तम्भपर्यन्तं परमात्मस्वरूपकम् ।
स्थावरं जंगमं चैव प्रणमामि जगन्मयम् ॥१५६॥

156. Everything here from Brahma down to a pillar is the form of Parmatman. Whatever is here in the entire world, moving and unmoving (knowing them to be Para Brahman), I prostrate.

वन्देहं सच्चिदानन्दं भावातीतं जगद्गुरुम् ।
नित्यं पूर्णं निराकारं निर्गुणं स्वात्मसंस्थितम् ॥१५७॥

157. I prostrate to the World-Teacher, who is Satchidananda (Existence-Knowledge-Bliss Absolute), who is above the different states of existence, etc., eternal, all-full, attributeless, formless and ever centred in the Self.

परात्परतरं ध्यायेन्नित्यमानन्दकारकम् ।
हृदयाकाशमध्यस्थं शुद्धस्फटिकसन्निभम् ॥१५८॥

158. One should ever meditate on the Supreme, beyond which nothing exists, which bestows bliss at all times (on one and all), which is seated in the heart-space and which shines pure as a crystal.

स्फाटिके स्फाटिकं रूपं दर्पणे दर्पणो यथा ।
तथात्मनि चिदाकारमानन्दं सोऽहमित्युत ॥१५९॥

159. Just as a crystal shines with all its beauty in a crystal, as a mirror in a mirror, so also, in the Self shines the bliss of the Chidakasa. "That I am" is beyond all doubts.

अंगुष्ठमात्रं पुरुषं ध्यायेच्च चिन्मयं हृदि ।
तत्र स्फुरति यो भाव: शृणु तत्कथयामि ते ॥१६०॥

160. Lord Siva says to Parvati: I shall tell you, O Parvati, the Bhava that arises in the heart when the Purusha, of the size of the thumb, is meditated upon as the Chinmaya in the heart.

*Notes*: Bhava is the state of consciousness. Chinmaya is all-pervading knowledge and light.

अजोऽहममरोऽहं च ह्यनादिनिधनो ह्यहम् ।
अविकारश्चिदानन्दो ह्यणीयान् महतो महान् ॥१६१॥

161. I am unborn. I am deathless. I am beginningless. I am endless. I am attributeless. I am consciousness and bliss. I am smallest of the small. I am the greatest of the great.

अपूर्वमपरं नित्यं स्वयंज्योतिर्निरामयम् ।
विरजं परमाकाशं ध्रुवमानन्दमव्ययम् ॥१६२॥

162. There is none prior to me and none later. I am eternal. I am self-effulgent. I am painless and diseaseless. I am ever-pure. I am the eternal Akasa (ether). I am without the least movement. I am bliss (Ananda) (imperishable, unchangeable or changeless is the idea).

अगोचरं तथाऽगम्यं नामरूपविवर्जितम् ।
नि:शब्दं तु विजानीयात्स्वभावाद्ब्रह्म पार्वति ॥१६३॥

163. O Parvati! I am the unseen. I am unreachable by speech and mind. I am without name and form. I am inexpressible by word or speech directly. Know me thus. For, this is my natural state of Being.

*Notes:* Verses 161, 162 and 163 give us the method of meditation on the Self. For the Self can never be an object, so, it cannot be expressed directly by mind or speech and taught or realised as *Idam* or this. It is always *Tat* or that and can be realised only as our Atman or Self as I. I am Brahman, *Aham Brahmasmi, So'ham* or *Om* only. There is no other way.

यथा गन्धस्वभावत्वं कर्पूरकुसुमादिषु ।
शीतोष्णत्वस्वभावत्वं तथा ब्रह्मणि शाश्वतम् ॥१६४॥

164. Just as smell is inherent and natural with camphor, flowers, etc., just as heat and cold are natural with fire and ice, so also, in Brahman eternity is natural. (Brahman is changeless and permanent).

यथा निजस्वभावेन कुण्डलकटकादयः ।
सुवर्णत्वेन तिष्ठन्ति तथाऽहं ब्रह्म शाश्वतम् ॥१६५॥

165. Just as gold exists in its own nature in ornaments like earrings, bangles, etc., so also, I am ever-permanent Brahman.

स्वयं तथाविधो भूत्वा स्थातव्यं यत्रकुत्रचित् ।
कीटो भृङ्ग इव ध्यानाद्यथा भवति तादृशः ॥१६६॥

166. Just as a worm by the constant fear of the black bee becomes a black bee itself ultimately, so also, one should by constant meditation practised on Brahman anywhere should become Brahman.

गुरुध्यानं तथा कृत्वा स्वयं ब्रह्ममयो भवेत् ।
पिण्डे पदे तथा रूपे मुक्तास्ते नात्र संशयः ।।१६७।।

167. One should, by practising meditation on the Guru, become Brahmamaya (attain Brahmic consciousness) while in this body (staying here itself) and attain the highest state of emancipation. Such a person is a freed soul. There is no doubt about this.

### ।। श्रीपार्वती उवाच ।।

पिण्डं किं तु महादेव पदं किं समुदाहृतम् ।
रूपातीतं च रूपं किं एतदाख्याहि शंकर ।।१६८।।

168. Parvati said: O Mahadeva, O Sankara, please tell me what is Pinda, what is Pada, what is Rupa and what is Rupatita.

### ।।श्रीमहादेव उवाच।।

पिण्डं कुण्डलिनी शक्तिः पदं हंसमुदाहृतम् ।
रूपं बिन्दुरिति ज्ञेयं रूपातीतं निरञ्जनम् ।।१६९।।

169. Sri Mahadeva said: Pinda is the Kundalini Sakti, Pada is said to be Hamsa, Rupa is Bindu and Rupatita is the attributeless (Niranjana).

*Notes*: Kundalini is the primordial energy coiled up in the Muladhara Chakra, the first of the six Chakras. Its seat is near about the Guda (anus). Hamsa is Jivatma here. Rupa is the Turiya state. Rupatita is the Turiyatita or the attributeless.

पिण्डे मुक्ताः पदे मुक्ता रूपे मुक्ता वरानने ।
रूपातीतं तु ये मुक्तास्ते मुक्ता नात्र संशयः ।।१७०।।

170. They are really free who are freed in Pinda. They are freed in Pada as well. They are freed in Rupa also. Those who are freed in Rupatita they are really free. There is no doubt about this, O Parvati.

*Notes:* Rupatita is above names and forms and the highest state of realisation. Here all Vasanas and Karmas are burnt. This verse hints that all kinds of realisation are real and lead to the highest. There is no inferior or superior in realisation. There is a gradual ascent and final Mukti. There is no going down from many of these stages.

गुरोध्यानेनैव नित्यं देही ब्रह्ममयो भवेत् ।
स्थितश्च यत्र कुत्रापि मुक्तोऽसौ नात्र संशय: ॥१७१॥

171. By constant meditation on the Guru alone, an embodied soul becomes the disembodied Brahman. Wherever he may stay, he is free. There is no doubt in this.

*Notes:* The force on the word "Dhyanenaiva" goes to show that the meditator on the Guru needs no other kind of meditation or object of meditation for his emancipation.

ज्ञानं स्वानुभव: शान्तिर्वैराग्यं वक्तृता धृति:
षड्गुणैश्वर्ययुक्तो हि भगवान् श्रीगुरु: प्रिये ॥१७२॥

172. Knowledge of the Self, Self-realisation, peace, dispassion, oratory and courage—the one possessing these six qualities is Bhagavan who is Sri Guru, my dear Parvati.

*Notes:* The first line of this verse has an alternative rendering: *"Jnanam vairagyam-aisvaryam yasah sri samudahritam"* which means knowledge, dispassion, lordliness, fame and wealth make up the qualities of the Guru Bhagavan.

गुरु: शिवो गुरुर्देवो गुरुर्बन्धु: शरीरिणाम् ।
गुरुरात्मा गुरुर्जीवो गुरोरन्यत्र विद्यते ।।१७३।।

173. Guru is Siva. Guru is God. Guru is the relative of all embodied beings. Guru is the Atman. Guru is Jiva. There is nothing other than the Guru.

एकाकी निस्पृह: शान्तश्चिन्तासूयादिवर्जित: ।
बाल्यभावेन यो भाति ब्रह्मज्ञानी स उच्यते ।।१७४।।

174. Alone, desireless, cool, peaceful, free from jealousy, greed, etc., one who maintains himself thus in reality, is a Brahma Jnani.

*Notes*: Balya Bhava is the state of enlightenment of a sage. Balya, Mouna and Panditya are the states of a realised saint. He is childlike in his simplicity. He is a Mouni who speaks only when necessary. He is well read. He is free from doubts.

न सुखं वेदशास्त्रेषु न सुखं मन्त्रयन्त्रके ।
गुरो: प्रसादादन्यत्र सुखं नास्ति महीतले ।।१७५।।

175. There is no happiness in anything in this world; not even in the Vedas, the Sastras, the Mantras, the Tantras even, except in the Grace of the Guru (Guru Prasada).

*Notes:* Prasada in the ordinary sense means the food-leavings of the Guru or the Lord. In the spiritual sense one should have the grace of the Guru (Guru-Kripa) which is capable of giving Mukti to the aspirant *"Moksha-mulam Guroh Kripa"*. This is hinted here and not merely the physical leavings *'Ucchishta'*.

चार्वाकवैष्णवमते सुखं प्राभाकरे न हि।
गुरो: पादान्तिके यद्वत्सुखं वेदान्तसम्मतम् ॥१७६॥

176. There is no real happiness in the philosophy of the Charvakas, nor of the Vaishnavas nor even of the Prabhakaras. The happiness present in the feet of the Guru is found nowhere else. This is an admitted fact in Vedanta.

*Notes*: Charvakas are those who take the body as the object of worship and say: "Eat, drink and be merry." Vaishnavas worship Lord Vishnu. Prabhakaras are followers of Mimamsa philosophy, the philosophy expounded by Kumarila Bhatta. This is one of the six Darshanas in Indian Philosophy.

न तत्सुखं सुरेन्द्रस्य न सुखं चक्रवर्तिनाम्।
यत्सुखं वीतरागस्य मुनेरेकान्तवासिन: ॥१७७॥

177. The happiness that is enjoyed by a saint free from all attachments, living in seclusion, is not enjoyed even by Indra, Lord of the Devas, or an emperor, or mighty rulers.

*Notes*: This is an echo of the gradation of bliss given in the Brahmananda Valli of the Taittiriya Upanishad which says that the bliss enjoyed by the Sage of Self-realisation is not enjoyed by any one including gods, Yakshas, Kinnaras, etc.

नित्यं ब्रह्मरसं पीत्वा तृप्तो य: परमात्मनि।
इन्द्रं च मन्यते तुच्छं नृपाणां तत्र का कथा ॥१७८॥

178. Having drunk to the full Brahmarasa and satisfied in the Paramatman, the sages of realisation

consider Indra as a mere straw and then what to speak of ordinary kings of the world.

Notes: 'Rankam' is another version for 'Tuchham' in the second line.

यतः परमकैवल्यं गुरुमार्गेण वै भवेत् ।
गुरुभक्तिरतः कार्या सर्वदा मोक्षकांक्षिभिः ॥१७९॥

179. The seekers after Liberation should at all times develop Guru Bhakti, because by following the path shown by the Guru one attains the Supreme Auspiciousness and the Kaivalya state.

एक एवाद्वितीयोऽहं गुरुवाक्येन निश्चितः ।
एवमभ्यस्यता नित्यं न सेव्यं वै वनान्तरम् ॥१८०॥

180. "I am one and one alone without a second", whoever thus practises constant meditation as a result of the advice of the Guru with a firm determination, need not take recourse to a forest (for hard penances). (This itself is enough penance and Tapas.)

अभ्यासान्निमिषेणैव समाधिमधिगच्छति ।
आजन्मजनितं पापं तत्क्षणादेव नश्यति ॥१८१॥

181 By practice even for a very short period (Nimesha—the time required to wink the eyes), one attains the state of Samadhi. The sins accumulated from birth are destroyed instantaneously.

किमावाहनमव्यक्ते व्यापकं किं विसर्जनम् ।
अमूर्तौ च कथं पूजा कथं ध्यानं निरामये ॥१८२॥

182. O sinless one (Parvati), how should one invoke Him who is the unmanifested? How and where should one

do Visarjana (to put back in one's own place from where one has been invoked) for the All-pervading? How to worship or meditate on Him who is formless?

*Notes*: These forms of worship pertain to personal gods only. It is not possible to worship the unmanifested Brahman just as we do the Lord in the temple.

गुरुर्विष्णुः सत्त्वमयो राजसश्चतुराननः ।
तामसो रुद्ररूपेण सृजत्यवति हन्ति च ॥१८३॥

183. As the Rajasic Brahma, Guru creates this world, as the Sattvic Vishnu he protects it, and as the Tamasic Rudra he destroys the world.

स्वयं ब्रह्ममयो भूत्वा तत्परं चावलोकयेत् ।
परात्परतरं नान्यत् सर्वगं च निरामयम् ॥१८४॥

184. Endowed fully with the Brahmic consciousness one should perceive the Supreme, All-pervading, diseaseless and the one Paratpara and nothing else. (Paratpara is beyond everything.)

तस्यावलोकनं प्राप्य सर्वसंगविवर्जितः ।
एकाकी निस्पृहः शान्तः स्थातव्यं तत्प्रसादतः ॥१८५॥

185. Having attained a glimpse of that Supreme One, one should stay alone, freed from all contacts, without any attachment, peaceful, by Its grace.

लब्धं वाऽथ न लब्धं वा स्वल्पं वा बहुलं तथा ।
निष्कामेनैव भोक्तव्यं सदा सन्तुष्टमानसः ॥१८६॥

186. Whether one gets something or not, be it a little or be it a large quantity, one should always with a

contented heart enjoy (objects) without the least attachment.

सर्वज्ञपदमित्याहुर्देही सर्वमयो भुवि ।
सदानन्द: सदा शान्तो रमते यत्र कुत्रचित् ॥१८७॥

187. Becoming Sarvamaya (all-full) in this world the man who is ever in bliss, ever peaceful, lives happily anywhere and everywhere. This state is known as the state of Sarvajnatva (the state of knowing everything).

*Notes*: The self, being always the subject must always be omniscient, for everything else must appear to it as an object only.

यत्रैव तिष्ठते सोऽपि स देश: पुण्यभाजन: ।
मुक्तस्य लक्षणं देवि तवाग्रे कथितं मया ॥१८८॥

188. Wherever he (the freed soul) stays, that country is blessed and accrues all merits and is praiseworthy. Thus O Devi, I have told you the characteristics of a freed soul.

उपदेशस्त्वयं देवि गुरुमार्गेण मुक्तिद: ।
गुरुभक्तिस्तथात्यन्ता कर्तव्या वै मनीषिभि: ॥१८९॥

189. O Devi, this is the advice in the path of Guru-marga which is capable of bestowing Mukti. Therefore Guru Bhakti should be practised by all with great devotion and faith.

नित्ययुक्ताश्रय: सर्वो वेदकृत्सर्ववेदकृत् ।
स्वपरज्ञानदाता च तं वन्दे गुरुमीश्वरम् ॥१९०॥

190. Ever free, the support for all, the author of the Vedas, the author of the entire Vedas, the bestower of

knowledge on one and all, I worship that Guru who is himself God.

यद्यप्यधीता निगमाः षडंगा आगमाः प्रिये ।
अध्यात्मादीनि शास्त्राणि ज्ञानं नास्ति गुरुं विना ॥१९१॥

191. O beloved Parvati, one might have learnt the four Vedas and the six-branched Agamas (Siksha, Kalpa, Vyakarana, Nirukta, Jyotisha and Chhandas) and all Adhyatma Sastras; but one cannot attain knowledge without a Guru.

शिवपूजारतो वापि विष्णुपूजारतोऽथवा ।
गुरुतत्त्वविहीनश्चेत्तत्सर्वं व्यर्थमेव हि ॥१९२॥

192. One may be engaged in Siva Puja or deeply immersed in Vishnu Puja, but if he is without a knowledge of the Guru Tattva, all his learning is a mere waste.

शिवस्वरूपमज्ञात्वा शिवपूजा कृता यदि ।
सा पूजा नाममात्रं स्याच्चित्रदीप इव प्रिये ॥१९३॥

193. If worship of Siva is done without knowing the real nature of Siva, that worship is for the mere name's sake. My dear Parvati, that worship is like a lamp drawn on a paper.

*Notes*: Just as the picture of a lamp drawn on paper cannot illumine the dark room, so also worship of the Lord done without knowing His real Tattva is fruitless. Worship of sincere devotees is not meant here. Only worship done for outward show and popularity is discouraged. Since Puja is an essential need for knowing the Lord, it is not ruled out. The meaning is that one should do Puja with faith and devotion.

## SRI GURU GITA

सर्वं स्यात्सफलं कर्म गुरुदीक्षाप्रभावतः ।
गुरुलाभात्सर्वलाभो गुरुहीनस्तु बालिशः ॥१९४॥

194. By the glory and efficacy of Guru Diksha, all your actions bear fruit. By the attainment of a Guru, one attains everything. One without a Guru is a mere fool.

गुरुहीनः पशुः कीटः पतंगो वक्तुमर्हति ।
शिवरूपं स्वरूपं च न जानाति यतस्स्वयम् ॥१९५॥

195. Since one does not understand the nature of Siva and one's own Self by himself, one without a preceptor can be said to be a mere animal, worm or firefly.

*Notes:* One without a Guru is devoid of discrimination and wastes one's life like an animal, a worm or a firefly.

तस्मात्सर्वप्रयत्नेन सर्वसंगविवर्जितः ।
विहाय शास्त्रजालानि गुरुमेव समाश्रयेत् ॥१९६॥

196. Therefore discarding all kinds of contacts with people, by all possible means, giving up all conflicts of the scriptures, one should depend on the Guru only.

*Notes*: Depending on the Guru includes wholehearted service and following his instructions to the very letter.

निरस्तसर्वसन्देहो एकीकृत्य सुदर्शनम् ।
रहस्यं यो दर्शयति भजामि गुरुमीश्वरम् ॥१९७॥

197. Devoid of all doubts, with one-pointed and concentrated Vision of the Supreme, whoever reveals the secrets and makes the supreme Vision possible, to that Lord and Guru, I pay my worship.

ज्ञानहीनो गुरुस्त्याज्यो मिथ्यावादी विडम्बक: ।
स्वविश्रान्तिं न जानाति परंशान्तिं करोति किम्॥१९८॥

198. The Guru devoid of knowledge, who indulges in falsehood and who is full of vanity, is not able to find peace for himself. How is he to bestow peace on others?

शिलाया: किं परं ज्ञानं शिलासंघप्रतारणे ।
स्वयं तर्तुं न जानाति परं निस्तारयेत् कथम् ॥१९९॥

199. What special knowledge has a stone in saving other stones from drowning? It cannot go across the river by itself and how can it help other stones to go across?

न वन्दनीयास्ते कष्टं दर्शनाद्भ्रान्तिकारका: ।
वर्जयेत्तान् गुरुन् दूरे धीरानेव समाश्रयेत् ॥२००॥

200. They (such Gurus) are not at all fit to be worshipped. How painful it is? By a mere look they create delusion. Such Gurus should be abandoned from a distance. One should depend upon the brave and learned ones.

पाषण्डिन: पापरता: नास्तिका भेदबुद्धय: ।
स्त्रीलम्पटा दुराचारा: कृतघ्ना बकवृत्तय: ॥२०१॥

कर्मभ्रष्टा: क्षमानष्टा निन्द्यतर्कैश्च वादिन: ॥
कामिन: क्रोधिनश्चैव हिंसाश्चण्डा: शठास्तथा ॥२०२॥

ज्ञानलुप्ता न कर्तव्या महापापास्तथा प्रिये ।
एभ्यो भिन्नो गुरु: सेव्य: एकभक्त्या विचार्य च ॥२०३॥

201, 202, 203. O Parvati, imposters and non-believers in the Vedas, habitual sinners, atheists, slaves of women, evil-doers, traitors, religious hypocrites, those fallen from the Karma Marga (path shown by the Vedas), those who are impatient, who indulge in vain discussions, sensualists, those who are angry, violent, unyielding to reasoning, devoid of knowledge, great sinners—such Gurus should be avoided; and one should take refuge under real teachers with one-pointed devotion and discrimination.

शिष्यादन्यत्र देवेशि न वदेद्स्य कस्यचित् ।
नराणां च फलप्राप्तौ भक्तिरेव हि कारणम् ॥२०४॥

204. O Devi, this should not be revealed to anyone other than the disciple. Devotion is the cause for the attainment of desired fruits by men.

*Notes:* Faith and devotion play a very significant role in the attainment of knowledge, Bhakti (devotion) and even Mukti.

गूढो दृढश्च प्रीतिश्च मौनेन सुसमाहित: ।
सकृत्कामगतौ वापि पञ्चधा गुरुरीरित: ॥२०५॥

205. The hidden, the firm, the loving and contented, the silently concentrated, the one who wanders at his will and suddenly and unexpectedly turns up to bless a Sishya, out of his abundant mercy, of his own accord—these are the five kinds of teachers.

सर्वं गुरुमुखाल्लब्धं सफलं पापनाशनम् ।
यद्यदात्महितं वस्तु तत्तद्द्रव्यं न वञ्चयेत् ॥२०६॥

206. Whatever is received from the Guru (by way of instructions, admonitions, etc.,) is fruitful and is capable of destroying sins, and is in his best interests. The disciple should never defraud the wealth of the Guru.

गुरुदेवार्पणं वस्तु तेन तुष्टोऽस्मि सुव्रते ।
श्रीगुरो: पादुकां मुद्रां मूलमन्त्रं च गोपयेत् ।।२०७।।

207. O good lady, I am satisfied with whatever things are offered to the Guru by the disciple. The sandals, the seals and the Mulamantra (Guru Mantra)—these should be kept hidden.

नतास्मि ते नाथ पदारविन्दं
बुद्धिन्द्रियप्राणमनोवचोभि: ।
यच्चिन्त्यते भावित आत्मयुक्तौ
मुमुक्षुभि: कर्ममयोपशान्तये ।।२०८।।

208. Parvati said: I adore O Lord, Thy Lotus Feet, that are always thought of in full concentration by earnest seekers who wish to free themselves from the effect of their own actions, through words, mind, Prana, the intellect and all the senses.

अनेन यद्भवेत्कार्यं तद्ददामि तव प्रिये ।
लोकोपकारकं देवि लौकिकं तु विवर्जयेत् ।।२०९।।

209. Mahadeva said: I shall tell you, O Parvati, what can be achieved by this. This I narrate to you for the benefit of the world. One should shun all wrorldliness from one's mind.

लौकिकाद्धर्मतो याति ज्ञानहीनो भवार्णवे ।
ज्ञानभावे च यत्सर्वं कर्म निष्कर्म शाम्यति ।।२१०।।

210. One devoid of knowledge in this ocean of Samsara undergoes a lot of sufferings. In the state when one acquires knowledge of the Self, both Karma and Nishkarma become nullified.

# SRI GURU GITA

इमां तु भक्तिभावेन पठेद्वै शृणुयादपि ।
लिखित्वा यत्प्रदानेन तत्सर्वं फलमश्नुते ॥२११॥

211. Whoever studies this with faith and devotion, or hears (with devotion), or writes in a book and makes a gift of it to someone, attains all merits.

गुरुगीतामिमां देवि हृदि नित्यं विभावय ।
महाव्याधिगतैर्दुःखैः सर्वदा प्रजपेन्मुदा ॥२१२॥

212. O Devi, may you meditate on this Guru Gita in your heart with great devotion. Even when you are faced with the sufferings on account of incurable diseases (Mahavyadhi), you should repeat this with cheerfulness of heart.

गुरुगीताक्षरैकैकं मन्त्रराजमिदं प्रिये ।
अन्ये च विविधा मन्त्राः कलां नार्हन्ति षोडशीम् ॥२१३॥

213. O dear Parvati, every letter and syllable of this Guru Gita is each a Mantra-Raja (king among Mantras). Other Mantras, manifold in nature, do not deserve the credit of even one sixteenth part of this.

अनन्तफलमाप्नोति गुरुगीताजपेन तु ।
सर्वपापहरा देवि सर्वदारिद्र्यनाशिनी ॥२१४॥

214. One acquires endless fruits by the repetition of the Guru. It destroys all sins, O Devi, and it removes all poverty.

अकालमृत्युहर्त्री च सर्वसंकटनाशिनी ।
यक्षराक्षसभूतादिचोरव्याघ्रविघातिनी ॥२१५॥

215. The study of Guru Gita puts an end to untimely

death and all afflictions. It destroys also the evil effects of Yakshas, Rakshasas, Bhutas, fear of thieves, tigers, etc.

सर्वोपद्रवकुष्ठादिदुष्टदोषनिवारिणी ।
यत्फलं गुरुसान्निध्यात्तत्फलं पठनाद्भवेत् ॥२१६॥

216. The study of Guru Gita removes all afflictions, troubles, diseases like leprosy and great sins. By the study of Guru Gita one derives the benefit of the holy company of the Guru.

*Notes:* One who is away from his Guru can, by the study of Guru Gita, acquire the benefit of the Guru's presence with him.

महाव्याधिहरा सर्वविभूतेः सिद्धिदा भवेत् ।
अथवा मोहने वश्ये स्वयमेव जपेत्सदा ॥२१७॥

217. This Guru Gita becomes the bestower of all Siddhis (occult powers) and all divine Aisvaryas and remover of all kinds of diseases. In cases of Mohana and Vasya (illusive powers) one should always do Japa of this Gita.

*Notes:* Mohana is deluding others, Vasya is keeping others in submission to one's will. One can use Guru Gita for nullifying the effect of Mohana and Vasya practised by others. With its help one can practise these also.

कुशदूर्वासने देवि ह्यासने शुभ्रकम्बले ।
उपविश्य ततो देवि जपेदेकाग्रमानसः ॥२१८॥

218. Seated on a mat of Kusa or Durva grass or a seat made of white blanket, one should repeat the Japa with one-pointedness and concentration of mind.

शुक्लं सर्वत्र वै प्रोक्तं वश्ये रक्तासनं प्रिये ।
पद्मासने जपेन्नित्यं शान्तिवश्यकरं परम् ॥२१९॥

219. A white seat is recommended for all purposes. Red colour is used for Vasya. One should sit in the Padma (lotus) pose and do Japa for acquiring peace supreme.

वस्त्रासने च दारिद्र्यं पाषाणे रोगसम्भव: ।
मेदिन्यां दु:खमाप्नोति काष्ठे भवति निष्फलम् ॥२२०॥

220. If the Japa is done sitting on a seat made of cloth, one gets poverty; disease, if seated on a stone; if seated on the ground, pain accrues; and if seated on a wooden seat, one accrues no fruit or the effort goes in vain.

कृष्णाजिने ज्ञानसिद्धिर्मोक्षश्रीर्व्याघ्रचर्मणि ।
कुशासने ज्ञानसिद्धि: सर्वासिद्धस्तु कम्बले ॥२२१॥

221. If seated on deer-skin one attains Jnana, and if seated on tiger-skin one attains Moksha. If seated on Kusha-grass-seat one gets knowledge of the Self, and if seated on woollen seat one acquires all psychic powers.

आग्नेय्यां कर्षणं चैव वायव्यां शत्रुनाशनम् ।
नैर्ऋत्यां दर्शनं चैव ईशान्यां ज्ञानमेव च ॥२२२॥

222. By doing Japa facing South-East one gets powers to attract others, facing North-West one will have no enemies, facing South-West one will have vision (of God) and facing North-East one acquires knowledge.

उदङ्मुख: शान्तिजप्ये वश्ये पूर्वमुखस्तथा ।
याम्ये तु मारणं प्रोक्तं पश्चिमे च धनागम: ॥२२३॥

223. Facing North during Japa one becomes peaceful, facing East one will attract others, facing South one meets with death and facing West one acquires plenty of wealth.

मोहनं सर्वभूतानां बन्धमोक्षकरं परम् ।
देवराज्ञां प्रियकरं राजानं वशमानयेत् ।।२२४।।

224. This Guru Mantra has the power to attract all. It destroys all bonds and causes freedom. It makes Indra favourable to you. It brings under your control even kings.

मुखस्तम्भकरं चैव गुणानां च विविर्धनम् ।
दुष्कर्मनाशनं चैव तथा सत्कर्मसिद्धिदम् ।।२२५।।

225. This Mantra has the power to stop one's power of speech. It increases one's virtues. It destroys all evil Karmas and intensifies good actions.

*Notes:* The tendency to do good and desist from evil Karmas is meant here.

असिद्धं साधयेत्कार्यं नवग्रहभयापहम् ।
दु:स्वप्ननाशनं चैव सुस्वप्नफलदायकम् ।।२२६।।

226. One attains success in all actions including those which are considered unsuccessful. It is the remover of the fear of the evil influences of the planets. It totally destroys all evil dreams and bestows the fruit of good Karmas.

*Notes:* The Phala Sruti mentioned here in these verses applies equally to Guru Kripa, Guru Mantra Japa and Guru Gita Japa.

मोहशान्तिकरं चैव बन्धमोक्षकरं परम् ।
स्वरूपज्ञाननिलयं गीताशास्त्रमिदं शिवे ।।२२७।।

227. O auspicious one, this Gita Sastra brings peace where there is confusion and restlessness. It brings freedom from all bonds. It Is the storehouse of all knowledge and particularly Atma Jnana.

यं यं चिन्तयते कामं तं तं प्राप्नोति निश्चयम् ।
नित्यं सौभाग्यदं पुण्यं तापत्रयकुलापहम् ।।२२८।।

228. Whatever desire a man has or thinks of that he gains. It bestows eternal goodwill, fortune and holiness and destroys the three kinds of pains (Adhyatmic, Adhibhautic and Adhidaivic) root and branch.

सर्वशान्तिकरं नित्यं तथा वन्ध्यासुपुत्रदम् ।
अवैधव्यकरं स्त्रीणां सौभाग्यस्य विवर्धनम् ।।२२९।।

229. This bestows all peace and permanent happiness like that enjoyed by a barren woman getting a Suputra (a son who is obedient and well behaved). For women this Guru Gita is the giver of all fortune and Avaidhavya (the state of non-widowhood).

आयुरारोग्यमैश्वर्यं पुत्रपौत्रप्रवर्धनम् ।
निष्कामजापी विधवा पठेन्मोक्षमवाप्नुयात् ।।२३०।।

230. One attains health, long life, prosperity, increase in sons, grandsons, etc. A widow who studies this without any selfish end in view attains salvation.

अवैधव्यं सकामा तु लभते चान्यजन्मनि ।
सर्वदुःखमयं विघ्नं नाशयेत्तापहारकम् ।।२३१।।

231. A widow who studies this with expectation of worldly fruits will, in other births, never become a widow. It destroys all her pains, fears, obstacles and afflictions.

सर्वपापप्रशमनं धर्मकामार्थमोक्षदम् ।
यं यं चिन्तयते कामं तं तं प्राप्नोति निश्चितम् ॥२३२॥

232. This is a destroyer of all sins. It bestows Dharma, desires, wealth and liberation. He certainly attains all objects of his desires.

काम्यानां कामधेनुर्वै कल्पते कल्पपादपः ।
चिन्तामणिश्चिन्तितस्य सर्वमंगलकारकम् ॥२३३॥

233. Of all desires for objects Guru Gita is Kamadhenu. Of things thought of in the mind it is Kalpataru (wish-yielding tree). Of all things desired for, it is Chintamani Jewel creative of all auspiciousness.

*Notes*: Kamadhenu, Kalpavriksha and Chintamani—these, capable of yielding whatever is wished for, are available to the inhabitants of heaven.

लिखित्वा पूजयेद्यस्तु मोक्षश्रियमवाप्नुयात् ।
गुरुभक्तिर्विशेषेण जायते हृदि सर्वदा ॥२३४॥

234. Whoever writes the whole Guru Gita with hand and offers worship to it attains Moksha. In his heart will arise always particular devotion to the Guru.

जपन्ति शाक्ताः सौराश्च गाणपत्याश्च वैष्णवाः
शैवाः पाशुपताः सर्वे सत्यं सत्यं न संशयः ॥२३५॥

235. Guru Gita is repeated by the followers of Sakti, followers of Lord Surya, followers of Lord Ganapati, followers of Lord Vishnu and followers of Lord Siva, all

alike, with equal devotion. This is the Truth. This is the Truth. There is absolutely no doubt in this.

इति श्रीस्कान्दोत्तरखण्डे सनत्कुमारसंहितायां
उमामहेश्वरसंवादे श्रीगुरुगीतायां द्वितीयोऽध्यायः ॥

Thus ends the second chapter of the Guru Gita, being a dialogue between Sri Uma and Sri Mahesvara (Parvati and Siva), which forms a part of the Sanat Kumara Samhita, in the Uttarakhanda of the Skanda Purana.

# CHAPTER III

अथ काम्यजपस्थानं कथयामि वरानने ।
सागरान्ते सरित्तीरे तीर्थे हरिहरालये ॥ २३६ ॥

शक्तिदेवालये गोष्ठे सर्वदेवालये शुभे
वटस्य धात्र्या मूले वा मठे वृन्दावने तथा ॥ २३७ ॥

पवित्रे निर्मले देशे नित्यानुष्ठानतोऽपि वा ।
निर्वेदनेन मौनेन जपमेतत् समारभेत् ॥ २३८ ॥

**236, 237, 238.** Now I shall tell, O Good Lady, (Lord Siva says to Parvati) the suitable places where Guru Gita can be recited with the intention of achieving one's own desired objects. Seashore, near any river, any place of pilgrimage, temples of Vishnu or Siva or Devi, cowsheds, all temples, underneath a Vata Vriksha (banyan tree), Vrindavana (forest of Vrinda trees), or in any pure place, Japa of Guru Gita can be undertaken. One should commence the Japa of this Guru Gita after performing one's daily obligatory duties, observing silence and with a pure dispassionate heart.

जाप्येन जयमाप्नोति जप सिद्धिं फलं तथा ।
हीनं कर्म त्यजेत्सर्वं गर्हितस्थानमेव च ॥ २३९ ॥

**239.** By doing this Japa one attains success and Japa Siddhi undoubtedly. One should abandon all forbidden acts and also renounce forbidden places.

श्मशाने बिल्वमूले वा वटमूलान्तिके तथा ।
सिद्ध्यन्ति कानके मूले चूतवृक्षस्य सन्निधौ ॥२४०॥

240. One should do the Japa in cremation grounds, under a Bilva tree or a Vata tree or a Kanaka tree or a mango tree for attainment of success.

पीतासनं मोहने तु ह्यासितं चाभिचारिके ।
ज्ञेयं शुक्लं च शान्त्यर्थं वश्ये रक्तं प्रकीर्तितम् ॥२४१॥

241. The practitioner should have yellow seat in cases of Mohana, white seat for attaining peace and red-coloured seats in cases of Vasya.

जपं हीनासनं कुर्वत् हीनकर्मफलप्रदम् ।
गुरुगीतां प्रयाणे वा संग्रामे रिपुसंकटे ॥२४२॥

जपन् जयमवाप्नोति मरणे मुक्तिदायिका ।
सर्वकर्माणि सिद्ध्यन्ति गुरुपुत्रे न संशयः ॥२४३॥

242, 243. By doing Japa sitting on a forbidden seat, one attains the fruit of forbidden acts. One attains success. By doing Japa in deathbed one attains liberation. By repeating Guru Gita at the time of undertaking a journey, in fights, and when faced with fear of enemies, one attains success. To him all acts give the desired fruits, and undoubtedly so, for the Guru Putra (son of the Guru).

गुरुमन्त्रो मुखे यस्य तस्य सिद्ध्यन्ति नान्यथा ।
दक्षया सर्वकर्माणि सिद्ध्यन्ति गुरुपुत्रके ॥२४४॥

244. To the person, who has always the Guru Mantra on his tongue, all acts become fruitful, otherwise not. By

the power of initiation one attains success in all Karmas (acts) and particularly in the case of a Guruputraka (disciple).

*Notes*: In reality the disciple is the real son of the Guru.

भवमूलविनाशाय चाष्टपाशनिवृत्तये ।
गुरुगीताम्भसि स्नानं तत्त्वज्ञ: कुरुते सदा ॥२४५॥

245. For the destruction of Samsara root and branch and for the destruction of the eight kinds of attachments, the knower of Truth takes bath in the waters of the Guru Gita.

*Notes*: This verse indicates that the real Ganga is the Guru Gita waters.

स एव सद्गुरु: साक्षात् सद्सद्ब्रह्मवित्तम: ।
तस्य स्थानानि सर्वाणि पवित्राणि न संशय: ॥२४६॥

246. He is the real Guru, Sadguru, who is the knower of the Sat and Asat (what is Truth and what is untruth). All his places are holy. There is not even an iota of doubt.

सर्वशुद्ध: पवित्रोऽसौ स्वभावाद्यत्र तिष्ठति ।
तत्र देवगणा: सर्वे क्षेत्रपीठे चरन्ति च ॥२४७॥

247. Wherever the ever-pure Guru stays of his own accord, there all the Devas (gods) stay. They move about the place of residence of the Guru.

*Notes*: The residence of the Guru becomes the dwelling place of Devas and therefore it becomes heaven.

आसनस्था: शयाना वा गच्छन्तस्तिष्ठन्तोऽपि वा ।
अश्वारूढा गजारूढा: सुषुप्ता जाग्रतोऽपि वा ॥२४८॥

## SRI GURU GITA

शुचिभूता ज्ञानवन्तो गुरुगीतां जपन्ति ये ।
तेषां दर्शनसंस्पर्शात् दिव्यज्ञानं प्रजायते ॥२४९॥

248, 249. One attains knowledge by the sight or touch of those pure souls endowed with wisdom who repeat Guru Gita while seated, lying, moving, standing, mounted on horseback, or elephant back, waking or sleeping. (The last portion of verse 249 has another version *"Punar janma na vidyate"*—to them there is no rebirth.)

समुद्रे वै यथा तोयं क्षीरे क्षीरे जले जलम् ।
भिन्ने कुम्भे यथाकाशं तथाऽऽत्मा परमात्मनि ॥२५०॥

तथैव ज्ञानवान् जीव: परमात्मनि सर्वदा ।
ऐक्येन रमते ज्ञानी यत्र कुत्र दिवानिशम् ॥२५१॥

एवंविधो महायुक्त: सर्वत्र वर्तते सदा ।
तस्मात्सर्वप्रकारेण गुरुभक्तिं समाचरेत् ॥२५२॥

250, 251 & 252. The Atman becomes one with the Paramatman just as river water becomes one with the water in the ocean, milk with milk, water with water or pot-ether with Mahakasa. So also, the man of knowledge lives in constant union with the Supreme all day and night. Thus united with Maha Yoga he exists in all places at all times. Therefore, by all means one should practise Guru-Bhakti.

गुरुसन्तोषणादेव मुक्तो भवति पार्वति ।
अणिमादिषु भोक्तृत्वं कृपया देवि जायते ।२५३।

253. O Parvati, one becomes free by pleasing the

Guru. By his grace one becomes entitled to enjoy the eightfold Siddhis (Anima, Mahima, etc.)

साम्येन रमते ज्ञानी दिवा वा यदि वा निशि ।
एवंविधो महामौनी त्रैलोक्यसमतां व्रजेत् ॥ २५४ ॥

254. The Jnani remains in and enjoys the bliss of equanimity, be it day or night. Thus the Maha Mouni acquires the state of equanimity in the three worlds.

*Notes*: Nothing disturbs the Jnani, in whichever state he is kept in or in whatever work he engages himself induced by Prarabdha. One whose mind delights in Brahman, is simply in a state of ecstasy. There is nothing like pain for him. *"Yasya Brahmani ramate chittam nandati nandati nandatyeva"*—that is his state.

अथ संसारिण: सर्वे गुरुगीताजपेन तु ।
सर्वान् कामांस्तु भुञ्जन्ति त्रिसत्यं मम भाषितम् ॥२५५॥

255. By the recitation again and again of Guru Gita the people of the world (Samsaris) will attain all their desired objects. Whatever I have said, O Parvati, is true. It is true. It is true. (Repetition is for emphasis.)

सत्यं सत्यं पुन: सत्यं धर्मसारं मयोदितम् ।
गुरुगीतासमं स्तोत्रं नास्ति तत्त्वं गुरो: परम् ।२५६॥

256. It is Truth. It is Truth. It is nothing but the Truth. Whatever is declared by me in this connection is the essence of virtue. There is no prayer equal to Guru Gita and there is no truth greater than the Guru Tattva.

गुरुदेवो गुरुर्धर्मो गुरौ निष्ठा परं तप: ।
गुरो: परतरं नास्ति त्रिवारं कथयामि ते ॥२५७॥

257. Guru is God. Guru is Dharma. The greatest penance is unshakable faith in Guru. There is nothing superior to Guru. I repeat it thrice with force.

धन्या माता पिता धन्यो गोत्रं धन्यं कुलोद्भव:
धन्या च वसुधा देवि यत्र स्याद्गुरुभक्तता ॥२५८॥

258. Blessed is the mother, blessed is the father and blessed is the family and tradition, blessed the Earth, O Devi, where there is Guru Bhakti.

आकल्पजन्मकोटीनां यज्ञव्रततप:क्रिया: ।
ता: सर्वा: सफला देवि गुरुसन्तोषमात्रत: ॥२५९॥

259. O Devi, by the mere satisfaction of the Guru, all penances, sacrifices, austerities, etc., practised in crores of births, in crores of Kalpas (world process) become fruitful.

शरीरमिन्द्रियं प्राणश्चार्थ: स्वजनबन्धुता ।
मातृकुलं पितृकुलं गुरुरेव न संशय ॥२६०॥

260. The body, the senses, the vital airs, wealth, one's own relatives, the mother's clan, the father's clan—all those are present in one's Guru. There is not the least doubt about this.

मन्दभाग्या ह्यशक्ताश्च ये जना नानुमन्वते ।
गुरुसेवासु विमुखा: पच्यन्ते नरकेऽशुचौ ॥२६१॥

261. The unfortunate, the weak, those who have turned their faces against the service of the Guru, who do not avail the opportunity of service of the Guru—these persons suffer in terrible hells.

विद्या धनं बलं चैव तेषां भाग्यं निरर्थकम् ।
येषां गुरुकृपा नास्ति अधो गच्छन्ति पार्वति ॥२६२॥

ब्रह्मा विष्णुश्च रुद्रश्च देवता: पितृकिन्नरा: ।
सिद्धचारणयक्षाश्च अन्ये च मुनयो जना: ॥२६३॥

262, 263. Learning, wealth, strength, high fortune—all these are of no use without the grace of Guru. Even if one has attained the status of Brahma, Vishnu, Rudra, the Gods, the Pitris, the Kinnaras, the Siddhas, the Charanas, the Yakshas or even great Rishis, (without Guru-Kripa) he falls down.

गुरुभाव: परं तीर्थमन्यतीर्थं निरर्थकम् ।
सर्वतीर्थमयं देवि श्रीगुरोश्चरणाम्बुजम् ॥२६४॥

264. Guru-Bhava (the status of the Guru) is the greatest purifier or Tirtha (holiest of the holies). Others are worthless. All Tirthas are present, O Devi, in the sacred holy feet of the Guru.

*Notes*: By Guru-Bhava is meant the spirit of reverent adoration to the Guru, as realised by the Sishya, by virtue of his having become his Sishya.

कन्याभोगरता मन्दा: स्वकान्ताया: पराङ्मुखा: ।
अत: परं मया देवि कथितन्न मम प्रिये ॥२६५॥

265. Those who are averse to their legally wedded wives and indulge in enjoying with other women (including their own daughters), are fools and thoughtless men of beastly nature. O Devi, I am giving out these great Truths to you, so that even such people may improve by developing devotion to the Guru.

इदं रहस्यमस्पष्टं वक्तव्यं च वरानने ।
सुगोप्यं च तवाग्रे तु ममात्मप्रीतये सति ॥२६६॥

266. This great secret, difficult to understand (not clear on the face of it) should not be revealed to all. It is to be kept well guarded. I have related this to you because you are very dear to me.

स्वामिमुख्यगणेशाद्यान् वैष्णवादींश्च पार्वति ।
न वक्तव्यं महामाये पादस्पर्शं कुरुष्व मे ॥२६७॥

267. This should not be revealed to any one including Ganesha, Subrahmanya, even the gods, or even the Vaishnavas, O Mahamaye. Give me this assurance by touching my feet, O Devi.

अभक्ते वञ्चके धूर्ते पाषण्डे नास्तिकादिषु ।
मनसाऽपि न वक्तव्या गुरुगीता कदाचन ॥२६८॥

268. To the devotionless, to the cheat, to the wicked, to the faithless, to the atheists and others of their type, this Guru Gita should never be told, not even mentally.

*Notes*: This should not be told even to those who think that too much praise of the Guru is done in this book. Even they are unfit to be told these top-secrets in Guru Tattva.

गुरवो बहव: सन्ति शिष्यवित्तापहारका: ।
तमेकं दुर्लभं मन्ये शिष्यहृत्तापहारकम् ॥२६९॥

269. There are ever so many teachers in the world who rob the wealth of their disciples. But I consider him (that Guru) a rare specimen among Gurus, who is able to remove the afflictions of the disciple's heart.

चातुर्यवान् विवेकी च अध्यात्मज्ञानवान् शुचि: ।
मानसं निर्मलं यस्य गुरुत्वं तस्य शोभते ।।२७०।।

270. The clever, the able, the discriminative, the pure, the knower of the Truths of the spiritual science, the one whose heart is pure, he is really the Guru. His Gurutva (the state of a Guru) shines, not of others.

*Notes*: Just as it is difficult to find a true disciple, so also it is equally hard to find a really qualified Guru.

गुरवो निर्मला: शान्ता: साधवो मितभाषिण: ।
कामक्रोधविनिर्मुक्ता सदाचारा: जितेन्द्रिया: ।।२७१।।

271. Preceptors (Gurus) are those who are pure at heart, calm and collected, who speak measured words, who are free from lust, greed, hatred, etc., who have conquered their senses and who are established in Sadachara.

सूचकादिप्रभेदेन गुरवो बहुधा स्मृता: ।
स्वयं सम्यक् परीक्ष्यार्थ तत्त्वनिष्ठं भजेत्सुधी: ।।२७२।।

272. Teachers are of various types with different capacities; they are known by names, Suchaka, etc. The student should know and test for himself and serve the one who is established in Tattva Nishtha (knowledge of the Self).

*Notes*: Who is Suchaka Guru is explained in the next verse.

वर्णजालमिदं तद्बुद्बाह्यशास्त्रं तु लौकिकम् ।
यस्मिन् देवि समभ्यस्तं स गुरु: सूचक: स्मृत: ।।२७३।।

273. The Suchaka teacher is one who is well-versed in letters and all external worldly sciences.

वर्णाश्रमोचितां विद्यां धर्माधर्मविधायिनीम् ।
प्रवक्तारं गुरुं विद्धि वाचकं त्वति पार्वति ।।२७४।।

274. O Parvati, know the instructor of the duties of the different castes and orders—Varna and Ashrama—Dharma, Adharma, etc., to be of the Vachaka type.

पंचाक्षर्यादिमन्त्राणामुपदेष्टा तु पार्वति ।
स गुरुर्बोधको भूयादुभयोरयमुत्तम: ।।२७५।।

275. The Guru who initiates the disciple into the Panchakshari Mantra, etc., O Parvati, he is of the Bodhaka type and he is superior to both (the Suchaka and Vachaka type) named above.

मोहमारणवश्यादितुच्छमन्त्रोपदर्शिनम् ।
निषिद्धगुरुरित्याहु: पण्डितास्तत्त्वदर्शिन: ।।२७६।।

276. The Guru who initiates one into the lower type of Vidyas like the Mohana, Marana, Ucchatana, Vasya, etc., him the Panditas, the knowers and seers of Truth, call by the name Nishiddha Guru.

अनित्यमिति निर्दिश्य संसारं संकटालयम् ।
वैराग्यपथदर्शी य: स गुरुर्विहित: प्रिये ।।२७७।।

277. "Everything here is transitory and an abode of calamities" viewing thus the world which is an abode of miseries, the Guru, who shows the path leading to Vairagya (dispassion), is known as the Vihita type.

तत्त्वमस्यादिवाक्यानामुपदेष्टा तु पार्वति ।
कारणाख्यो गुरु: प्रोक्तो भवरोगनिवारक: ॥२७८॥

278. The teacher who initiates the disciple into the Mahavakyas, Tattvamasi, etc., O Parvati, he is called by the name Karana Guru. He removes the disease of Samsara in the disciple.

सर्वसन्देहसन्दोहनिर्मूलनविचक्षण: ।
जन्ममृत्युभयघ्नो य: स गुरु: परमो मत: ॥२७९॥

279. He who is an expert in the removal of multitudes of doubts root and branch, and who removes the fear of birth and death, is considered to be the Parama Guru.

बहुजन्मकृतात् पुण्याल्लभ्यतेऽसौ महागुरु: ।
लब्ध्वाऽमुं न पुनर्याति शिष्य: संसारबन्धनम् ॥२८०॥

280. One gets such a Mahaguru as the result of merits acquired in many births. Having attained such a Guru, the disciple is never again bound to the Samsara. He becomes absolutely free.

एवं बहुविधा लोके गुरव: सन्ति पार्वति ।
तेषु सर्वप्रयत्नेन सेव्यो हि परमो गुरु: ॥२८१॥

281. O Parvati, there are in this world many kinds of teachers. Of all these one should by all means and efforts serve the Parama Guru. He is fit to be served.

निषिद्धगुरुशिष्यस्तु दुष्टसंकल्पदूषित: ।
ब्रह्मप्रलयपर्यन्तं न पुनर्याति मर्त्यताम् ॥२८२॥

282. The disciple of a Nishiddha Guru impelled by evil

and wicked desires of a harmful nature, never again gets a human body till the close of a Brahma Pralaya.

*Notes*: Brahma Pralaya takes place after two lakhs of Divine years.

एवं श्रुत्वा महादेवी महादेववचस्तथा ।
अत्यन्तविह्वलमना शंकरं परिपृच्छति ॥२८३॥

283. Hearing the words of Mahadeva, Parvati (Mahadevi) asked thus with a greatly distressed mind.

*॥ पार्वत्युवाच ॥*

नमस्ते देवदेवात्र श्रोतव्यं किंचिदस्ति मे ।
श्रुत्वा त्वद्वाक्यमधुना भृशं स्याद्विह्वलं मनः ॥२८४॥

284. Sri Parvati said: O Lord, I prostrate to you. There is something which I have to hear from you. My mind is rather confused and agitated by hearing your words.

स्वयं मूढा मृत्युभीताः सुकृताद्विरतिं गताः ।
दैवान्निषिद्धगुरुगा यदि तेषां तु का गतिः ॥२८५॥

285. I want to ask you the fate of those disciples who by chance (ordained by fate) approach a Nishiddha Guru. They are by themselves not endowed with much discrimination, but the force of their own meritorious deeds attain Virakti and are afraid of death. (Please enlighten me.)

*॥ श्री महादेव उवाच ॥*

शृणु तत्त्वमिदं देवि यदा स्याद्विरतो नरः ।
तदाऽसावधिकारीति प्रोच्यते श्रुतिमस्तकैः ॥२८६॥

286. Sri Mahadeva said: O Devi, hear this Truth. When one is endowed with Vairagya (disgust for worldly enjoyments and household life), the Srutis say that he is a proper Adhikari (qualified student).

अखण्डैकरसं ब्रह्म नित्यमुक्तं निरामयम् ।
स्वस्मिन् सन्दर्शितं येन स भवेदस्य देशिक: ॥२८७॥

287. One who enables the student to see within himself the one homogeneous essence that is the ever-free, free from pain, the immortal Brahman, becomes his saviour and teacher.

जलानां सागरो राजा यथा भवति पार्वति ।
गुरुणां तत्र सर्वेषां राजायं परमो गुरु: ॥२८८॥

288. Just as the ocean is the king of waters, so also, such a supreme teacher (Parama Guru) becomes the king among all teachers.

मोहादिरहित: शान्तो नित्यतृप्तो निराश्रय: ।
तृणीकृतब्रह्मविष्णुवैभव: परमो गुरु: ॥२८९॥

289. A Parama Guru is one who is devoid of Moha, etc., peaceful, always contented in himself, not depending on any one else, who considers as mere straw the status of Brahma (the creator) and Vishnu even.

सर्वकालविदेशेषु स्वतन्त्रो निश्चलस्सुखी ।
अखण्डैकरसास्वादतृप्तो हि परमो गुरु: ॥२९०॥

290. One who is independent at all times and climes, who possesses an unshakable mind and ever happy, who enjoys the Akhandaikarasa (the homogeneous essence)

of the Atman and is satisfied in it—such a one is a Parama Guru.

दैताद्वैतविनिर्मुक्तः स्वानुभूतिप्रकाशवान् ।
अज्ञानान्धतमश्छेत्ता सर्वज्ञः परमो गुरुः ॥२९१॥

291. One who is free from the feeling of Dvaita and Advaita, who shines by the light of his Self-realisation, who is able to destroy the deep darkness of ignorance, and who is an All-Knower—he is a Parama Guru.

यस्य दर्शनमात्रेण मनसः स्यात् प्रसन्नता ।
स्वयं भूयात् धृतिश्शान्तिः स भवेत् परमो गुरुः ॥२९२॥

292. By whose mere Darsan (look) one attains calmness, cheerfulness, and peace of mind as also Dhriti— such a one is a Parama Guru.

सिद्धिजालं समालोक्य योगिनां मन्त्रवादिनाम् ।
तुच्छाकारमनोवृत्तिर्यस्यासौ परमो गुरुः ॥२९३॥

293. Beholding the network of Siddhis of the Yogis and the Mantravadins (those who deal with the wonders of Mantras), one who has the determination "all this is nothing but straw"—such a person is a Parama Guru.

स्वशरीरं शवं पश्यन् तथा स्वात्मनमद्वयम् ।
यः स्त्रीकनकमोहघ्नः स भवेत् परमो गुरुः ॥२९४॥

294. One who looks upon his own body as a corpse, and his own Self as the non-dual Brahman, and who has killed ruthlessly the infatuation for wealth and women, such a person is a Parama Guru.

मौनी वाग्मीति तत्त्वज्ञो द्विधाभूच्छृणु पार्वति ।
न कश्चिन्मौनिनां लाभो लोकेऽस्मिन्भवति प्रिये ॥२९५॥

295. O Parvati, listen to me. There are two classes of knowers of Truth (Tattvajnas). They are (1) the Mouni and (2) the Vagmi.

*Notes:* No profit accrues from a Mouni to any person in this world, for he does not express or teach to others, being silent and not inclined to speak out or help others, being absorbed in his own self.

वाग्मी तूत्कटसंसारसागरोत्तारणक्षमः ।
यतोऽसौ संशयच्छेत्ता शास्त्रयुक्त्यनुभूतिभिः ॥२९६॥

296. The Vagmi is on the other hand capable of saving others from the great whirlpool of Samsara Sagara (the ocean of birth and death). Therefore, he is able to clear the doubts of all by his knowledge of the Sastras, his own cogent arguments which are always convincing and by his own direct realisation (Anubhava Jnana), and knowledge of the self.

*Notes*: Refer to *Sri Sankara Vijaya* (IV-60) Ajnanantar-gahanapatitan etc.—to make this point clear.

गुरुनामजपाद्देवि बहुजन्मार्जितान्यपि ।
पापानि विलयं यान्ति नास्ति सन्देहमण्वपि ॥२९७॥

297. By the Japa of the Guru's name, O Devi, the sins acquired in countless lives are destroyed. There is not the least doubt about this.

श्रीगुरोस्सदृशं दैवं श्रीगुरोस्सदृशः पिता ।
गुरुध्यानसमं कर्म नास्ति नास्ति महीतले ॥२९८॥

298. In this world, there is no God like the Sri Guru and no father like the Sri Guru. There is no act equal to Guru Dhyana (meditation on the Guru) in this world. Undoubtedly there is no act like this; nothing like this.

कुलं धनं बलं शास्त्रं बान्धवास्सोदरा इमे ।
मरणे नोपयुज्यन्ते गुरुरेको हि तारक: ॥२९९॥

299. Family traditions, wealth, strength, the knowledge of the Sastras, relatives, brothers—none of these is useful to you at the time of death. Guru is the only saviour.

कुलमेव पवित्रं स्यात् सत्यं स्वगुरुसेवया ।
तृप्ता: स्युस्सकला देवा ब्रह्माद्या गुरुतर्पणात् ॥३००॥

300. By the service of the Guru, truly the entire family is purified. By the satisfaction of the Guru, all the Devas, Brahma, Vishnu, Siva, etc., become pleased.

गुरुरेको हि जानाति स्वरूपं देवमव्ययम् ।
तज्ज्ञानं तत्प्रसादेन नान्यथा शास्त्रकोटिभि: ॥३०१॥

301. It is only the Guru who knows the real Svarupa (nature) of the Imperishable Lord. The knowledge of the Supreme is by his grace (Guru's) and there is no other way. Even through thousands or crores of scriptures one cannot attain that knowledge.

*Notes*: Avyayam means unchanging or changeless, for it is above Maya and continues to be same in nature.

स्वरूपज्ञानशून्येन कृतमप्यकृतं भवेत् ।
तपोजपादिकं देवि सकलं बालजल्पवत् ॥३०२॥

302. Without a knowledge of the Self (Svarupa),

whatever is done becomes fruitless. O Devi, penance, Japa of Mantras, etc., everything becomes like the prattling of a child.

शिवं केचिद्द्वरिं केचिद्द्विधिं केचित्तु केचन ।
शक्तिं देवमिति ज्ञात्वा विवदन्ति वृथा नरा: ॥३०३॥

303. Some say Siva is the Supreme Lord, some hold Hari to be the greatest. Others say Brahma is all this and some say this is all Sakti Lila. Holding different views, they argue here without any purpose.

न जानन्ति परं तत्त्वं गुरुदीक्षापराङ्मुखा: ।
भ्रान्ता: पशुसमा होते स्वपरिज्ञानवर्जिता: ॥३०४॥

304. Those who are averse to Guru Diksha (initiation) never know the supreme truth. They are like mere animals and mad without the knowledge of the Self.

तस्मात्कैवल्यसिद्ध्यर्थं गुरुमेव भजेत्प्रिये ।
गुरुं विना न जानन्ति मूढास्तत्परमं पदम् ॥३०५॥

305. For the attainment of emancipation from the cycle of birth and death, therefore, you should propitiate your Guru, O Dear Parvati. Without a Guru, the ignorant ones of the world cannot know the Supreme Reality.

भिद्यते हृदयग्रन्थिश्छिद्यन्ते सर्वसंशया: ।
क्षीयन्ते सर्वकर्माणि गुरो: करुणया शिवे ॥३०६॥

306. All the knots of the heart are rent asunder, all doubts are cleared, all the Karmas are destroyed by the grace and mercy of the Guru, O Parvati!

कृताया गुरुभक्तेस्तु वेदशास्त्रानुसारत: ।
मुच्यते पातकाद्घोराद्गुरुभक्तो विशेषत: ॥३०७॥

307. Guru Bhakti (devotion to Guru) practised according to the injunction of the Vedas and the Sastras by one devoted to the Guru, is capable of freeing one from all capital sins even.

दु:संगं च परित्यज्य पापकर्म परित्यजेत् ।
चित्तचिह्नमिदं यस्य तस्य दीक्षा विधीयते ॥३०८॥

308. One, who has abandoned bad company and also sinful acts, and who has a heart free from sins, to such a one Guru Diksha is ordained.

चित्तत्यागनियुक्तश्च क्रोधगर्वविवर्जित: ।
द्वैतभावपरित्यागी तस्य दीक्षा विधीयते ॥३०९॥

309. One, whose heart is fixed in Tyaga (renunciation), who is free from anger and pride, who has abandoned the feeling of all kinds of duality, to such a one Diksha is ordained.

एतल्लक्षण संयुक्तं सर्वभूतहितेरतम् ।
निर्मलं जीवितं यस्य तस्य दीक्षां विधीयते ॥३१०॥

310. One, who is endowed with these characteristics, who is interested in the welfare of all beings of the world, whose life is pure and untainted, to him is Diksha ordained by the Sastras.

क्रियया चान्वितं पूर्वं दीक्षाजालं निरुपितम् ।
मन्त्रदीक्षाभिधं सांगोपांग सर्वं शिवोदितम् ॥३११॥

311. The entire process of Diksha has been ordained

by me together with all rites and injunctions (says Lord Siva to Parvati) including the ordeal of Mantra Diksha together with the proper rites thereof.

क्रियया स्याद्विरहितां गुरुसायुज्यदायिनीम् ।
गुरुदीक्षां विना को वा गुरुत्वाचारपालकः ३१२

312. Without Guru Diksha, without the proper rites who can be said to be a follower of the injunctions of Guru Tattva which has the power of bestowing Guru Sayujya.

शक्तो न चापि शक्तो वा दैशिकांघ्रिसमाश्रयात् ।
तस्य जन्मास्ति सफलं भोगमोक्षफलप्रदम् ।।३१३।।

313. Whether qualified or not, one by unstinted devotion, and service to and refuge in the Guru becomes eligible for Moksha and enjoyment of all happiness here in this world. The life of such a disciple becomes fruitful.

अत्यंतचित्तपक्रस्य श्रद्धाभक्तियुतस्य च ।
प्रवक्तव्यमिदं देवि ममात्मप्रीतये सदा ।३१४।।

314. O Parvati, this should be revealed to one who is endowed with intense devotion and faith in the Guru, and who has purity of heart to the greatest degree. It gives me the greatest satisfaction and joy.

रहस्यं सर्वशास्त्रेषु गीताशास्त्रमिदं शिवे ।
सम्यक्परीक्ष्य वक्तव्यं साधकस्य महात्मनः ।।३१५।।

315. This Guru Gita Sastra is the secret of all scriptures, O Sive; to the high-souled Sadhaka this should be revealed after duly examining him.

सत्कर्मपरिपाकाच्च चित्तशुद्धस्य धीमत: ।
साधकस्यैव वक्तव्या गुरुगीता प्रयत्नत: ॥३१६॥

316. To the intelligent, to one possessed of Chitta Suddhi (purity of heart), to one in whom all good actions are fructifying, only to that qualified Sadhaka this Guru Gita should be imparted even with great effort.

नास्तिकाय कृतघ्नाय दांभिकाय शठाय च ।
अभक्ताय विभक्ताय न वाच्येयं कदाचन ॥३१७॥

317. To the atheist, to the deceitful, to one who does evil to one's well-wisher, to the cunning, to the hypocrite, to one who is not a devotee, to one opposed to the Guru,—this Guru Gita should never be told.

स्त्रीलोलुपाय मूर्खाय कामोपहतचेतसे ।
निन्दकाय न वक्तव्या गुरुगीता स्वभावत: ॥३१८॥

318. To the passionate, to one who craves for the constant company of ladies, to the wicked, whose mind is conquered by lust, desires, etc., to one who hates, naturally this Guru Gita should never be told.

सर्वपापप्रशमनं सर्वोपद्रववारकम् ।
जन्ममृत्युहरं देवि गीताशास्त्रमिदं शिवे ॥३१९॥

319. O Devi, O Sive, this Gita Sastra is the destroyer of all sins and remover of all evils and obstacles. It destroys the fear of birth and death.

श्रुतिसारमिदं देवि सर्वमुक्तं समासत: ।
नान्यथा सद्गति: पुंसां विना गुरुपदं शिवे ॥३२०॥

320. O Auspicious one, this is the essence of all Srutis (scriptures). In this everything has been said in a nutshell. There is no other way to the attainment of Mukti for people than devotion to the feet of Sadguru.

बहुजन्मकृतात्पापादयमर्थो न रोचते ।
जन्मबन्धनिवृत्यर्थं गुरुमेव भजेत्सदा ॥३२१॥

321. When an aspirant is weighed down by the sins of countless births, the real meaning of the Guru Gita does not appeal to him. To free oneself from the shackles of repeated births and deaths, one should devote oneself to the Guru only, at all times.

अहमेव जगत्सर्वं अहमेव परं पदम् ।
एतज्ज्ञानं यतो भूयात्तं गुरुं प्रणमाम्यहम् ॥३२२॥

322. "I am all this world, I am the supreme state of emancipation"—from whom one gets this kind of realisation (Knowledge), to that Guru, I ever prostrate.

अलं विकल्पैरहमेव केवलो
मयि स्थितं विश्वमिदं चराचरम् ।
इदं रहस्यं मम येन दर्शितं
स वन्दनीयो गुरुरेव केवलम् ॥३२३॥

323. Enough of all distractions. In reality I alone exist. In me the entire world of moving and unmoving objects rests. He (the Guru) who has revealed this secret to me really, he alone is fit to be worshipped.

यस्यान्तं नादिमध्यं न हि
करचरणं नामगोत्रं न सूत्रम् ।

नो जातिर्नैव वर्णो न भवति
पुरुषो नो नपुंसं न च स्त्री ॥३२४॥

नाकारं नो विकारं न हि जनिमरणं
नास्ति पुण्यं न पापम् ।
नोऽतत्त्वं तत्त्वमेकं सहजसमरसं
सद्गुरुं तं नमामि ॥३२५॥

324, 325. He who has neither end, middle nor beginning, who has neither hands, feet, caste, nor order, who is neither man, woman nor neuter (Napumsaka), who has neither change, birth, death, virtue, vice, who is neither Tattva—the only Truth, homogeneous, the same at all times, who is endowed with natural equanimity and uniform Bhava, to that Sat Guru I ever prostrate.

*Notes*: In reality, the Guru is beyond all dualities. He is the Supreme Brahman. He is free from all human elements and taints. He is in the enjoyment of Brahmic Bliss at all times.

नित्याय सत्याय चिदात्मकाय
नव्याय भव्याय परात्पराय ।
शुद्धाय बुद्धाय निरञ्जनाय
नमोऽस्तु नित्यं गुरुशेखराय ॥३२६॥

326. To the Eternal, to the ever-True, to the Conscious Light and Knowledge, to the ever-new, to the majestic dignified, to the Paratpara (greatest of the great), to the pure, to the enlightened, to the non-attached,—may this prostration be ever to that great Guru Sekhara (to the crest-jewel among teachers).

सच्चिदानन्दरूपाय व्यापिने परमात्मने ।
नमः श्री गुरुनाथाय प्रकाशानन्दमूर्तये ॥३२७॥

327. I ever prostrate to the Sri Gurunatha who is the all-pervading Paramatma whose form is Sat-chit-ananda (existence-knowledge-bliss), who is all light and bliss.

सत्यानन्दस्वरूपाय बोधैकसुखकारिणे ।
नमो वेदान्तवेद्याय गुरवे बुद्धिसाक्षिणे ॥३२८॥

328. I prostrate to the Guru who is the witness of my Buddhi, who is the knower of Vedanta (who can be known by Vedanta), whose form is truth and bliss (Satyananda Svarupa) and who is ever the cause of Knowledge and Bliss (Bodha and Sukha).

नमस्ते नाथ भगवन् शिवाय गुरुरूपिणे ।
विद्यावतारसंसिद्ध्यै स्वीकृतानेकविग्रह ॥३२९॥

329. Prostrations to Thee O Lord, O Bhagavan, Siva in Guru's form. You take various forms for the fulfilment of your Vidyavatara (spread of knowledge in the world).

नवाय नवरूपाय परमार्थैकरूपिणे ।
सर्वाज्ञानतमोभेदभावने चिद्घनाय ते ॥३३०॥

330. To the ever fresh and new who appears by His Maya, in various new, newer and newest forms (assumes), but yet who remains the only form of Paramartha (Reality), to the mass of pure consciousness or spiritual light, to the sun, the destroyer of all ignorance—be these prostrations.

स्वतन्त्राय दयाक्लृप्तविग्रहाय शिवात्मने ।
परतन्त्राय भक्तानां भव्यानां भव्यरूपिणे ॥ ३३१ ॥

विवेकिनां विवेकाय विमर्शाय विमर्शिनाम् ॥
प्रकाशिनां प्रकाशाय ज्ञानिनां ज्ञानरूपिणे ॥३३२॥

पुरस्तात्पार्श्वयो: पृष्ठे नमस्कुर्यादुपर्यध: ।
सदा मच्चित्तरूपेण विधेहि भवदासनम् ॥३३३॥

331, 332, 333. To the independent, to the image fashioned out of mercy, to the Siva Svarupa, to the refuge of devotees, to Him who is dependent on His Bhaktas, to the most beautiful form, to the discrimination of the Vivekis (those endowed with discrimination), to Him who is the enquiry in the equirers of Brahman, to the Light of lights, to Him who is light to those who need light, to Him who is the Knowledge of the Self in the Knowers of the Self, may these prostrations be in front, in back, above and below. May Thou be pleased to take Thy seat in my heart at all times. May You ever dwell in my heart.

श्रीगुरुं परमानन्दं वन्दे ह्यानन्दविग्रहम् ।
यस्य सन्निधिमात्रेण चिदानन्दाय ते मन: ॥३३४॥

334. Prostrations to Sri Guru who is supreme bliss, the form of Ananda, in whose presence (by whose mere presence) the mind assumes the form of pure consciousness and bliss.

नमोऽस्तु गुरवे तुभ्यं सहजानन्दरूपिणे ।
यस्य वागमृतं हन्ति विषं संसारसंज्ञकम् ॥३३५॥

335. May these prostrations be to thee O Guru, who

art ever immersed in natural bliss, and the nectar of whose speech destroys the poison called Samsara.

नानायुक्तोपदेशेन तारिता शिष्यसन्तति: ।
तत्कृपासारवेदेन गुरुचित्पदमच्युतम् ॥३३६॥

336. By innumerable suitable advices all your children-disciples have been saved. You have bestowed on them, by your extreme kindness, the imperishable state of Guruchitpadam.

अच्युताय नमस्तुभ्यं गुरवे परमात्मने ।
सर्वतन्त्रस्वतन्त्राय चिद्घनानन्दमूर्तये ॥३३७॥

337. Prostrations to Thee O Guru. You are the Paramatman. You are Achyuta (imperishable). You are well-versed in all the Sastras. You are Chidghana (mass of consciousness) and all Bliss.

*Notes:* Tantra here means Sastras. Svantantra means proficient, for all Sastric learning is in his Svadheena or Possession.

नमोऽच्युताय गुरवे विद्याविद्यास्वरूपिणे ।
शिष्यसन्मार्गपटवे कृपापीयूषसिन्धवे ॥३३८॥

338. Prostrations to Thee O Guru. You are Achyuta. Your form is both Vidya and Avidya. You are clever in putting your disciples on the right path. You are the ocean of nectar and mercy.

*Notes*: The second half of the first line of this verse has different version as—"*Ajnanadhvantaika-bhanave*"— meaning that the Guru is the one Sun who destroys the darkness of ignorance.

ओमच्युताय गुरुवे शिष्यसंसारसेतवे ।
भक्तकार्यैकसिंहाय नमस्ते चित्सुखात्मने ॥३३९॥

339. To the unfailing Guru, who helps the disciple in crossing the ocean of Samsara, becoming as it were, the bridge, the unfailing fulfiller of the devotees' works, prostrations to that Chitsukhatma (the unbounded joy that wells up in the heart).

गुरुनामसमं दैवं न पिता न च बान्धवाः ।
गुरुनामसमः स्वामी नेदृशं परमं पदम् ॥३४०॥

340. There is no God, no father not even any relative to equal Guru Nama (the name of the Guru). There is no Lord to equal Guru Nama. There is no status to equal this Parama Pada of the Guru.

एकाक्षरप्रदातारं यो गुरुं नैव मन्यते ।
श्वानयोनिशतं गत्वा चाण्डालेष्वपि जायते ॥३४१॥

341. He who does not respect and honour the Guru, the giver of the monosyllable, such a man takes innumerable births in detestable wombs like that of a dog and ultimately becomes a Chandala (goes to the Chandala Yoni).

गुरुत्यागाद्भवेन्मृत्युर्मन्त्रत्यागद्दरिद्रता ।
गुरुमन्त्रपरित्यागी रौरवं नरकं व्रजेत् ॥३४२॥

342. By abandoning one's Guru one goes to death, by renouncing the Mantra one endures poverty, the abandoner of Guru Mantra goes to the hell known as Raurava.

शिवक्रोधाद्गुरुस्त्राता गुरुक्रोधाच्छिवो न हि ।
तस्मात्सर्वप्रयत्नेन गुरोराज्ञां न लंघयेत् ।।३४३।।

343. Guru is able to save you from the anger of Siva. But even Siva cannot save you if you incur the displeasure and the anger of the Guru. Therefore, one should by all means and efforts take care to see that he does not disobey the orders of the Guru.

संसारसागरसमुद्धरणैकमन्त्रं
ब्रह्मादिदेवमुनिपूजितसिद्धमन्त्रम् ।
दारिद्र्यदुःखभवरोगविनाशमन्त्रं
वन्दे महाभयहरं गुरुराजमन्त्रम् ।।३४४।।

344. The Mantra that helps you to cross the ocean of Samsara, the Siddha Mantra that is worshipped by Brahma and perfected sages, the Mantra that saves you from poverty and from the great fear of Samsara, I prostrate to that great Gururaja Mantra.

सप्तकोटिमहामन्त्राश्चित्तविभ्रंशकारकाः ।
एक एव महामन्त्रो गुरुरित्यक्षरद्वयम् ।।३४५।।

345. The seven crores of Mahamantras cause mere restlessness to the mind. There is only one Mahamantra comprising of the two letters 'Gu' and 'Ru' (to save you).

एवमुक्त्वा महादेवः पार्वतीं पुनरब्रवीत् ।
इदमेव परं तत्त्वं शृणु देवि सुखावहम् ।।३४६।।

346. Having said this, Lord Mahadeva addressing Parvati again said these words: This is the one Supreme Tattva, O Devi, hear this; it will bestow on you all happiness.

गुरुतत्त्वमिदं देवि सर्वमुक्तं समासत: ।
रहस्यमिदमव्यक्तन्न वदेद्यस्य कस्यचित् ॥३४७॥

347. Thus the entire Guru Tattva has been said to you, O Devi, in a nutshell. This is a great unexpressed secret. Therefore, this should not be given to each and every one.

न मृषा स्यादियं देवि मदुक्ति: सत्यरूपिणी ।
गुरुगीतासमं स्तोत्रं नास्ति नास्ति महीतले ॥३४८॥

348. O Devi, this shall never become untrue. Whatever is said by me is true, O Satyarupini (an incarnation of Truth, the very form of Truth itself). There is no Stotra to equal this Guru Gita in the whole world. There is none. There is none.

गुरुगीतामिमां देवि भवदु:खविनाशिनीम् ।
गुरुदीक्षाविहीनस्य पुरतो न पठेत् क्वचित् ॥३४९॥

349. This Guru Gita is the dispeller of the pains of Samsara. O Devi, this should never be read out to one who has not got Guru Diksha (initiation from the Guru).

रहस्यमत्यन्तरहस्यमेतन्न
   पापिनां लभ्यमिदं महेश्वरि ।
अनेकजन्मार्जितपुण्यपाकाद्-
   गुरोस्तु तत्त्वं लभते मनुष्य: ॥३५०॥

350. This is a great secret. This secret of all secrets should not be given out to a sinner, O Devi. It is only by the virtuous deeds done in innumerable births fructifying in a person that he becomes eligible to get this great Truth.

यस्य प्रसादादहमेव सर्वं
मय्येव सर्वं परिकल्पितं च ।
इत्थं विजानामि सदात्मरूपं
तस्यांघ्रिपद्मं प्रणतोऽस्मि नित्यम् ॥३५१॥

351. By whose grace I realise now that "I am myself am everything and everything is superimposed on me", by whose grace I am able to know this Sadatmarupa (realise my own Self), to his Lotus Feet, I ever offer my worship and salutations.

अज्ञानतिमिरान्धस्य विषयाक्रान्तचेतस: ।
ज्ञानप्रभाप्रदानेन प्रसादं कुरु मे प्रभो ॥३५२॥

352. On me whose eyes are covered over by the cataract of ignorance, whose mind is captured by the pleasures of the senses, O Lord, by the gift of Jnana-Prabha (the light of knowledge) may Thy blessings be bestowed.

इति श्रीगुरुगीतायां तृतीयोऽध्याय: ।
इति श्रीस्कान्दोत्तरखण्डे सनत्कुमारसंहितायां
उमामहेश्वर संवादे श्रीगुरुगीता समाप्ता ॥

Thus ends the third chapter of the Guru Gita.

Thus ends the Guru Gita being a dialogue between Uma and Mahesvara, which forms a part of the Sanat Kumara Samhita in the Uttara Khanda of the Skanda Purana.

ॐ तत्सद्ब्रह्मणे नमः ।

## ॥ अथ ब्रह्मनामावली लिख्यते ॥

सकृच्छ्रवणमात्रेण ब्रह्मज्ञानं यतो भवेत् ।
ब्रह्मज्ञानावलीमाला सर्वेषां मोक्षसिद्धये ॥१॥

असंगोऽहमसंगोऽहमसंगोऽहं पुनः पुनः ।
सच्चिदानन्दरूपोऽहमहमेवाहमव्ययः ॥२॥

नित्यशुद्धविमुक्तोऽहं निराकारोऽहमव्ययः ।
भूमानन्दस्वरूपोऽहमहमेवाहमव्ययः ॥३॥

नित्योऽहं निरवद्योऽहं निराकारोऽहमच्युतः ।
परमानन्दरूपोऽहमहमेवाहमव्ययः ॥४॥

शुद्धचैतन्यरूपोऽहमात्मारामोऽहमेव च ।
अखण्डानन्दरूपोऽहमहमेवाहमव्ययः ॥५॥

प्रत्यक्चैतन्यरूपोऽहं शान्तोऽहं प्रकृतेः परः ।
शाश्वतानन्दरूपोऽहमहमेवाहमव्ययः ॥६॥

तत्त्वातीतः परात्माहं मध्यातीतः परः शिवः ।
मायातीतः परं ज्योतिरहमेवाहमव्ययः ॥७॥

नामरूपव्यतीतोऽहं चिदाकारोऽहमच्युतः ।
सुखरूपस्वरूपोऽहमहमेवाहमव्ययः ॥८॥

मायातत्कार्यदेहादि मम नास्त्येव सर्वदा ।
स्वप्रकाशैकरूपोऽहमहमेवाहमव्ययः ॥९॥

गुणत्रयमव्यतीतोऽहं ब्रह्मादीनां च साक्ष्यहम्।
अनन्तानन्दरूपोऽहमहमेवाहमव्यय: ।।१०।।

अन्तर्यामिस्वरूपोऽहं कूटस्थ: सर्वगोऽस्म्यहम्।
परमात्मस्वरूपोऽहमहमेवाहमव्यय: ।।११।।

निष्कलोऽहं निष्क्रियोऽहं सर्वात्माऽऽद्य: सनातन:।
अपरोक्षस्वरूपोऽहमहमेवाहमव्यय: ।।१२।।

द्वन्द्वादिसाक्षिरूपोऽहमचलोऽहं सनातन:।
सर्वसाक्षिस्वरूपोऽहमहमेवाहमव्यय: ।।१३।।

प्रज्ञानघन एवाहं विज्ञानघन एव च।
अकर्ताऽहमभोक्ताऽहमहमेवाहमव्यय: ।।१४।।

निराधारस्वरूपोऽहं सर्वाधारोऽहमेव च।
आप्तकामस्वरूपोऽहमहमेवाहमव्यय: ।।१५।।

तापत्रयविनिर्मुक्तो देहत्रयविलक्षण:।
अवस्थात्रयसाक्ष्यस्मि चाहमेवाहमव्यय: ।।१६।।

दृग्दृश्यौ द्वौ पदार्थौ स्त: परस्परविलक्षणौ।
दृग्ब्रह्म दृश्यं मायेति सर्ववेदान्तडिण्डिम: ।।१७।।

अहं साक्षीति यो विद्याद्विविच्यैवं पुन: पुन:।
स एव मुक्त: स विद्वानिति वेदान्तडिण्डिम: ।।१८।।

घटकुड्यादिकं सर्वं मृत्तिकामात्रमेव च।
तद्ब्रह्म जगत्सर्वमिति वेदान्तडिण्डिम: ।।१९।।

ब्रह्म सत्यं जगन्मिथ्या जीवो ब्रह्मैव नापर: ।
अनेन वेद्यं सच्छास्त्रमिति वेदान्तडिण्डिम: ।।२०।।

अन्तज्योंतिर्बहिज्योंति: प्रत्यग्ज्योति: परात्पर: ।
ज्योतिज्योंति: स्वयंज्योतिरात्मज्योति:
          शिवोऽस्म्यहम् ।।२१।।

इति श्रीमत्पमहंसपरिव्राजकाचार्य
श्रीशंकरभगवत्पादाचार्यविरचिता ब्रह्मनामावली समाप्ता ।।

## श्रीसद्गुरुपादुकास्तोत्रम्।

श्रीसमर्चितमव्ययं परमप्रकाशमगोचरं,
भेदवर्जितमप्रमेयमनन्तमाद्यमकल्मषम्।
निर्मलं निगमान्तमद्वयमप्रतर्क्यमबोधकं,
प्रातरेव हि मानसे गुरुपादुकाद्वयमाश्रये ।।१।।

नादबिन्दुकलात्मकं दशनादभेदविनोदकं,
मन्त्रराजविराजितं निजमण्डलान्तरभासितम्।
पञ्चवर्णमखण्डमद्भुतमादिकारणमच्युतं,
प्रातरेव हि मानसे गुरुपादुकाद्वयमाश्रये ।।२।।

व्योमवद्बहिरन्तरस्थितमक्षरं निखिलात्मकं,
केवलं परिशुद्धमेकमजन्म हि प्रतिरूपकम्।
ब्रह्मतत्त्वविनिश्चयं निरतानुमोक्षसुबोधकं,
प्रातरेव हि मानसे गुरुपादुकाद्वयमाश्रये ।।३।।

बुद्धिरूपमबुद्धिकं त्रितयैककूटनिवासिनं,
निश्चलं निखिलप्रकाशकनिर्मलं निजमूलकम्।
पश्चिमान्तरखेलनं निजशुद्धसंयमिगोचरं,
प्रातरेव हि मानसे गुरुपादुकाद्वयमाश्रये ।।४।।

हृद्गतं विमलं मनोज्ञविभासितं परमाणुकं,
नीलमध्यसुनीलसन्निभमादिबिन्दु निजांशुकम्।
सूक्ष्मकर्णिकमध्यमस्थितविद्युदादिविभासितं,
प्रातरेव हि मानसे गुरुपादुकाद्वयमाश्रये ।।५।।

पञ्च पञ्च हृषीकदेहमनश्चतुष्कपरस्परं,
पञ्चभौतिककामषट्कसमीरशब्दमुखेतरम्।

पञ्चकोशगुणत्रयादिसमस्तधर्मविलक्षणं,
प्रातरेव हि मानसे गुरुपादुकाद्वयमाश्रये ।।६।।

पञ्चमुद्रसुलक्ष्यदर्शनभावमात्रनिरूपणं,
विद्युदादिधगद्धगित्वरुचिर्विनोदविवर्धनम् ।
चिन्मुखान्तरवर्तिनं विलसद्द्विलासममायकं,
प्रातरेव हि मानसे गुरुपादुकाद्वयमाश्रये ।।७।।

पञ्चवर्णरुचिं विचित्रविशुद्धतत्त्वविचारणं,
चन्द्रसूर्यचिदग्निमण्डलमण्डितं घनचिन्मयम् ।
चित्कलापरिपूर्णमन्तरचित्समाधिनिरीक्षणं,
प्रातरेव हि मानसे गुरुपादुकाद्वयमाश्रये ।।८।।

हंसचारमखण्डनादमनेकवर्णमरूपकं,
शब्दजालमयं चराचरजन्तुदेहनिवासिनम् ।
चक्रराजमनाहतोद्भवमेकवर्णमतः परं,
प्रातरेव हि मानसे गुरुपादुकाद्वयमाश्रये ।।९।।

जन्मकर्मविलीनकारणहेतुभूतमभूतकं,
जन्मकर्मनिवारकं रुचिपूरकं भवतारकम् ।
नामरूपविवर्जितं निजनायकं शुभदायकं,
प्रातरेव हि मानसे गुरुपादुकाद्वयमाश्रये ।।१०।।

तप्तकाञ्चनदीप्यमानमहाणुमात्रमरूपकं,
चन्द्रिकान्तरतारकैरवमुज्ज्वलं परमास्पदम् ।
नीलनीरदमध्यमस्थितविद्युदादिविभासितं,
प्रातरेव हि मानसे गुरुपादुकाद्वयमाश्रये ।।११।।

स्थूलसूक्ष्मसकारणान्तरखेलनं परिपालनं,
विश्वतैजस प्राज्ञचेतसमन्तरात्मनिजांशुकम्।
सर्वकारणमीश्वरं निटिलान्तरालविदारकं,
प्रातरेव हि मानसे गुरुपादुकाद्वयमाश्रये ॥१२॥

इति श्रीमच्छंकराचार्यविरचितं श्रीसद्गुरुपादुकास्तोत्रम् सम्पूर्णम् ॥